180 Patchwork

Quilt Blocks

Experimenting with Colors, Shapes, and Styles to Piece New and Traditional Patterns

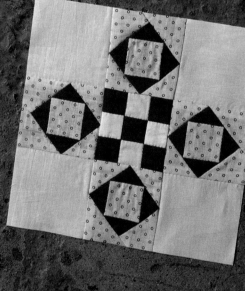

SUZUKO KOSEKI

About the Author

Suzuko Koseki is a quilt artist, fabric designer, chairwoman at La Clochette quilting school, and quilt instructor at Vogue Quilt Institute, Heart and Hands Patchwork School, and Asashi Culture Center. With an early background in fashion, she later discovered patchwork quilting, which has driven her successful career ever since. Her quilting style combines mature charm with a chic sensibility and has earned her many fans. She is a representative artist in the world of Japanese quilting. She has appeared in countless exhibitions has published numerous works, including *Natural Patchwork*, *Patchwork Style* and several other quilt titles. To learn more about Suzuko, visit her website at http://laclochette.jp

180 Patchwork Quilt Blocks

Landauer Publishing, www.landauerpub.com, is an imprint of
Fox Chapel Publishing Company, Inc.

IRO TO KATACHI PATCHWORK PATTERN DE NUNOASOBI
Suzuko Koseki
© 2020 Suzuko Koseki
© 2020 Graphic-sha Publishing Co., Ltd.
This book was first designed and published in Japan in 2020 by Graphic-sha Publishing Co., Ltd.
This English edition was published in 2022 by Fox Chapel Publishing
English translation rights arranged with Graphic-sha Publishing Co., Ltd.
through Japan Uni Agency, Inc., Tokyo

English Edition Project Team
Translator: Freire Disseny + Comunicació
Copy editor: Christa Oestreich
Designer: Mary Ann Kahn
Indexer: Jean Bissell

Japanese Edition Project Team
Creative cooperation: Etsuko Ikeda, Fumiko Kato, Naoko Sato, Eriko Sano, Naoko Taguchi,
    Keiko Miyamoto
Book design: Motoko Kitsukawa
Photos: Kazumasa Yamamoto
Drawing: Miyuki Oshima
Editing: Ayako Enaka (Graphic-sha Publishing Co., Ltd.)
Foreign edition production and management: Takako Motoki (Graphic-sha Publishing Co., Ltd.)

ISBN 978-1-947163-90-4

Library of Congress Control Number: 2022931717

We are always looking for talented authors. To submit an idea, please send a brief inquiry to acquisitions@foxchapelpublishing.com.

Note to Professional Copy Services:
The publisher grants you permission to make up to six copies of any quilt patterns in this book for any customer who purchased this book and states the copies are for personal use.

Printed in China
25 24 23 22   2 4 6 8 10 9 7 5 3 1

This book has been published with the intent to provide accurate and authoritative information in regard to the subject matter within. While every precaution has been taken in the preparation of this book, the author and publisher expressly disclaim any responsibility for any errors, omissions, or adverse effects arising from the use or application of the information contained herein.

41 Quilt Block Designs
80" x 89" (202 x 225cm)

Introduction

This volume is a collection of some of my favorite old patterns, old patterns I have slightly modified, and original patterns of mine. Furthermore, they all follow my own original color schemes. It mainly focuses on piecing patterns, but some of them require appliqué techniques. The shapes I use in these patterns have never lost their touch; they feel fresh no matter how many times you sew them. Classics that don't go old: squares, triangles, hexagons, and the Log Cabin quilt block. And thinking this should be a varied collection of patterns, I have included unique patterns that use fascinating shapes you might not have used very often, like curves, sharp angles, or circles, among others.

I have not organized the patterns in this book in a systematic manner, such as what you find in textbooks. Instead, I have divided them in a rough and free way into categories based on what they represent, what shapes they're made of, or what types of block they use.

I'd like to explain how you could search this book to find patterns you'd want to use. I imagine you'd first like to sew patterns you'd heard the name of, or you might feel like sewing a specific representation, like a flower. But how about you sew without thinking about what specific pattern you'd like to sew?

When browsing a pattern collection, the easiest is probably to choose patterns based on their overall impression. However, you may also choose patterns based on the specific shapes they use, such as triangles, circles, etc. Another way to clearly distinguish patterns is by the blocks that they're made up of. I divided my patterns in this simple way, based on their appearance, to make it easier for you to find the same pattern twice and sew it again. I feel a great number of patterns can be fit into these categories.

But what I consider to be the most crucial issue when sewing patterns is their color scheme. It brings great joy to any quilt maker, but also great distress. I recommend you use fabrics with designs and colors that you personally like. In my case, for the patterns that represent specific things, I used fabrics filled with designs. The strong contrasts between them made it easier to distinguish the pattern they create.

When I classified these patterns into groups, like "Mandalas" or "A Focus on Diagonal Lines," sections where they are lined up together, I tried to make the entire group work aesthetically, choosing pieces that would combine well together.

It's also thrilling to create something with the minimum amount of colors—just two.

First, it's best to draw the pattern and choose which fabric designs and colors you'd like to use. The same pattern can look entirely different depending on who sews it.

The color scheme is also what allows you to express your own inner world, all within these small patterns (often 7⅞" x 7⅞" [20 x 20cm]) constructed of all these small shapes. There's nothing like the joy you feel when you complete a pattern just as you'd imagined it.

The color schemes used in this book are but a tiny fraction of what you could do with these patterns. I hope that, thanks to them, you discover combinations of fabric designs and color that you hadn't thought of before. But there is no end to the shapes and colors in patchwork patterns.

I hope you enjoy creating with your favorite fabric designs and colors.

—**Suzuko Koseki**

Contents

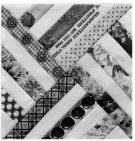

Index of Blocks

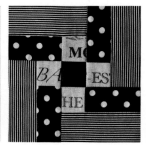

How to Use This Book

- This book is a collection of patterns organized into pages of one or two patterns per page. These are displayed both as an actual example made from fabric and a diagram. These not only show you how interesting the pattern shapes are on their own, but also give you ideas of which fabrics and colors you can use. The photographed examples measure 7⅞" x 7⅞" (20 x 20cm), with more complex patterns being 9½" x 9½" (24 x 24cm).

- These diagrams are included as a guide for you to make them yourself. You can use a ruler and a compass on graph paper to draw them. Starting on page 193, several pattern diagrams are included that might be harder to draw. A reduced diagram is shown for each, which you can photocopy at an enlarged resolution.

- It also includes several quilted items that are made from patterns in this book, so the design of these items is simply the patterns themselves. Be sure to use them as reference for creating your own quilted objects.

- Page 10 begins an explanation of how to quilt, and page 179 is the beginning of the instructions for the projects.

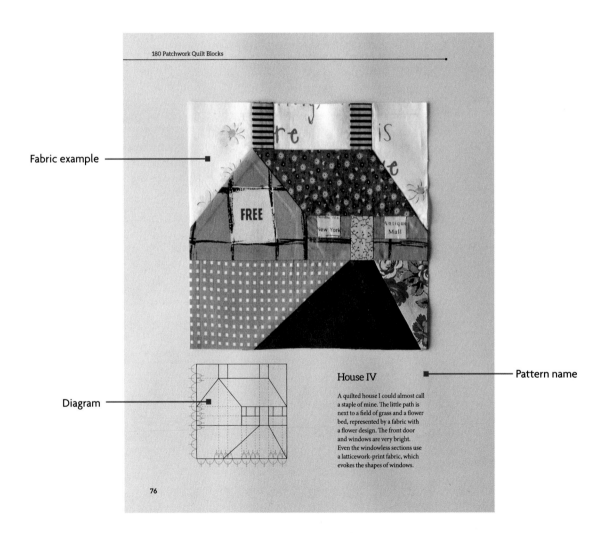

Fabric example

Diagram

Pattern name

180 Patchwork Quilt Blocks

House IV

A quilted house I could almost call a staple of mine. The little path is next to a field of grass and a flower bed, represented by a fabric with a flower design. The front door and windows are very bright. Even the windowless sections use a latticework-print fabric, which evokes the shapes of windows.

76

How to Draw Pattern Diagrams to Size

You can use the diagrams on each page as reference to draw your own.

1. Choose what size you'd like to use for the pattern, and draw a square of those proportions on graph paper.
2. Count how many lines are needed to divide the pattern into equal parts, and adapt the pattern's size to the amount of equal parts. For example, if a 7⅞" x 7⅞" (20 x 20cm) pattern were divided into six equal parts, you'd need to divide it into 1¼" (3.33cm) squares.
3. Draw guidelines for these divisions, connect the points of intersection between them, and create your diagram. The arrows show the radius of the circles. Place your compass on the center of the points of intersection to draw these circles. Any appliqué sections must be done after finishing the main piecing work.

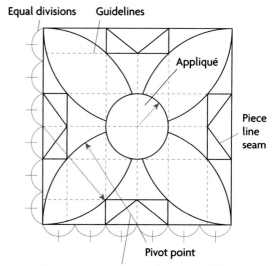

Equal divisions Guidelines

Appliqué

Piece line seam

Pivot point

The curve pattern line, or the radius of the guideline necessary for curves

How to Draw an Equilateral Pentagon

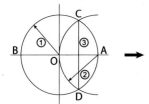

Draw two crossed lines, then draw a circle with O at the center. Now draw a half-circle with the A intersection at the center, which connects points C and D.

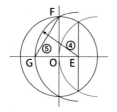

With E (the intersection between CD and the central line) at the center, draw a half-circle that crosses F (an intersection in circle 1). This half-circle should connect points F and G.

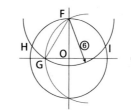

Use FG (whose size is equal to the sides of a hexagon) as the radius for a half-circle with F at the center.

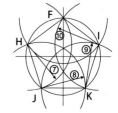

Draw an identical half-circle with H at the center, which creates a point of intersection at J in circle 1. Now draw the same half-circle with J at the center, and repeat this until it unites all points of intersection.

How to Draw an Equilateral Hexagon

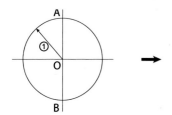

Draw two crossed lines, and draw a circle with O at the center.

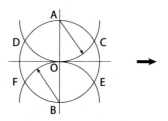

Draw half-circles with points A and B (the intersections between the central line and the circle) at the center, and make them both cross intersection O.

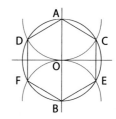

Connect all the intersections, and you're done.

How to Sew a Pattern

This will explain all the steps, from the creation of the pattern paper to the sewing of the pattern itself.

Making a Pattern Paper and Cutting the Fabric
The Mosaic pattern will serve as an example. We'll use a template sheet to make a pattern paper.

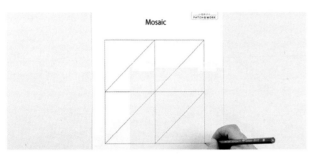

1. Add a template over the pattern's full-size diagram and attach it to the table to prevent it from moving. Use a pencil to draw dots to mark all the corners of the diagram.

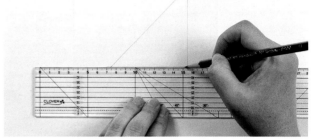

2. Remove the sheet from the diagram, and use a ruler to draw lines uniting all the dots. Make the squares extend beyond the dots you've drawn. The line extensions aid in adding seam allowances in step 5 and later anchoring your stitch line.

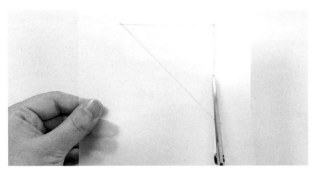

3. Use scissors to cut exactly at the marks. This will give you the pattern paper.

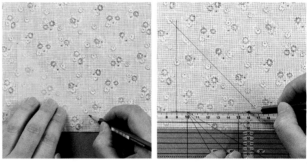

4. Place the cloth facedown on your cutting surface. Place your pattern paper over it and mark all the corner dots. Remove the pattern paper, and draw lines with a ruler from dot to dot. Here, too, you'll make the lines extend beyond the dots you've drawn.

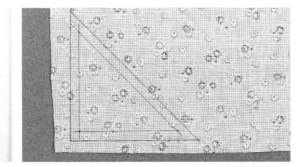

5. Add marks about ⁹⁄₃₂" (0.7cm) outside the main marks for the seam allowance. It helps if you use a patchwork ruler since they show ⁹⁄₃₂" (0.7cm) divisions.

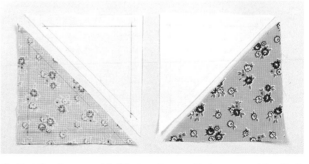

6. Cut the shapes with fabric scissors. Cut as many identical pieces as are necessary for your pattern.

Sewing Basics

The most basic sewing instructions for sewing from one edge of the cloth to another.

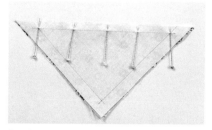

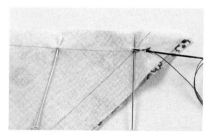

1. Take the connecting pieces and join right sides together, making the corner marks of one connect with the corner marks of the other. Use those marks to perpendicularly pierce both pieces with marking pins. Keep the pieces tightly positioned with your fingers and pierce a small amount of fabric, about ¹⁄₁₆" (0.2cm).

2. Place marking pins first at the edges, and then in the center. Since you added a ⁹⁄₃₂" (0.7cm) seam allowance when cutting the pieces, their edges now connect.

3. Insert the needle about two stitch positions behind the corner mark. When marking the fabric, you extended your line beyond the corner, so you can use that line now as a reference point. Begin by backstitching one stitch.

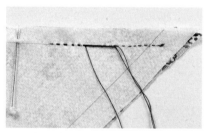

4. Follow the marks, making very small stitches along the way. Once you've reached back to a marking pin, you can remove it and continue.

5. Once you've sewn to the other edge, take the shrunken seam and extend it. If you're dealing with the cloth's bias, it will extend very easily, so take care to pull on it very softly while keeping the cloth in place.

6. Sew two stitches beyond the mark, backstitch, and make a French knot.

7. Press the stitches. Make sure it doesn't stretch the fabric.

8. Press open the block, in this case, a half-square triangle (HST), making the seam allowance rest on one side. Now, press the edge of the stitches.

9. Cut any seam allowance that extends outward. These are generally referred to as "tails."

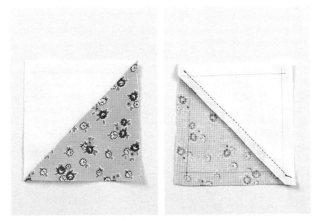

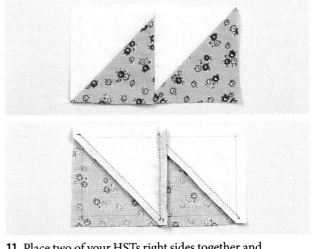

10. Half square triangle front and back; make four total to complete the block shown.

11. Place two of your HSTs right sides together and stitch join along the side edge as shown. Repeat with the second pair.

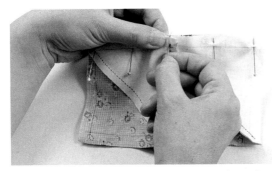

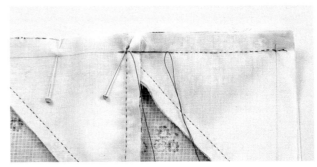

12. Right sides together, join the two units from the previous step. Place marking pins first on both edges, then in the center of one of the pieces, and then the center of the other piece. Even if the seams don't match perfectly here, we'll make them match once we start sewing.

13. Start by backstitching from the edge. Once you reach the seam, backstitch one stitch. Don't avoid the seam allowance; instead, sew them together.

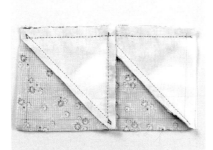

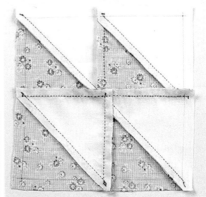

14. Continue sewing until two stitches beyond the mark, backstitch, and make a French knot. Press the seams as shown in steps 7 and 8, and make the seam allowance rest on one side.

15. Finished!

How to Do Inlay Sewing

A method for connecting the areas joining three pieces.

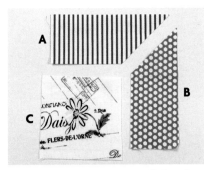

1. Prepare the pieces. You will do inlay sewing for the sections where the inside of the pieces touch. You will sew from the drawn pattern lines, not from the edges of the fabric.

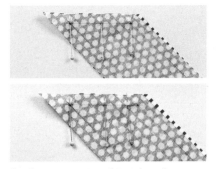

2. Place pieces A and B right sides together as shown, and place marking pins first on the edges and then on the center. The right-side edge will need inlaying, so we'll insert the pins more toward the left.

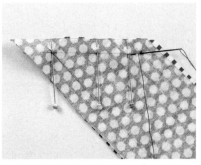

3. Insert your needle where your pattern line begins on the right, backstitch one stitch, and proceed with sewing.

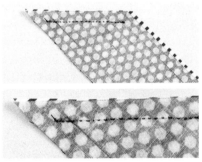

4. Finally, sew two stitches over the actual pattern line, backstitch, and make a French knot. The inlayed side will be the only one that requires you to sew from the actual pattern line and then toward the edge of the fabric.

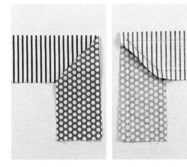

5. Unfold the pieces and make the seam allowance rest on one side. Then, press the seams to straighten them out.

6. Place the right side of piece C against the right side of the unit from step 5 so that the corner mark of piece C falls where your stitch line stopped on the unit. Pin.

7. Sew from the right side along the marked pattern line to the corner of piece C.

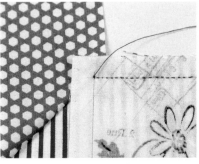

8. Make a small French knot at this mark. Use one cycle of thread to generate the French knot gap.

9. Turn the C piece around and fold it up with piece B. Align the marks on both pieces, and pin to secure.

13

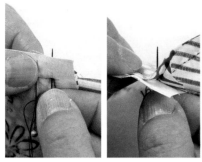

10. Continue sewing from the place you stopped in step 8. Insert the needle into the same spot, and thread the seam between pieces C and B, taking care not to fold piece A.

11. Backstitch one stitch and then proceed to sew to the edge.

12. Hold down the seam with an iron, and make the seam allowance rest on one side. This section is finished!

How to Sew Around a Center Square

A sewing method that circles around, making it hard to know where the sewing begins or where it ends.

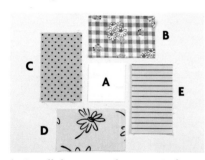

1. Cut all the required pieces. You're sewing a central square surrounded by rectangles. Make a mark where the seam allowances intersect at the upper right corner of piece A.

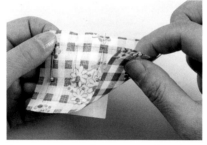

2. Position A and B pieces right sides together, aligning the upper left corner of A with the lower left corner of B as shown, and pin. You'll first place a pin on the mark you made in step 1 and then a pin on the left-side edge.

3. Start sewing from the space in between these two marking pins. Start sewing without backstitching, but finally backstitch once we've reached the edge. Unfold the pieces and press the seam allowance to the side of piece B.

4. Place piece C right sides together as shown with the AB unit from step 3; pin to secure. Then, sew from one edge to the other. Backstitch both at the start and at the end of the process.

5. Unfold the pieces, press them, and make the seam allowance rest on the side of piece C.

6. Place piece D right sides together against joined piece A/C as shown. Pin and stitch. Open and press with seam allowance against D.

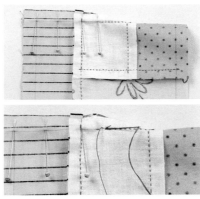

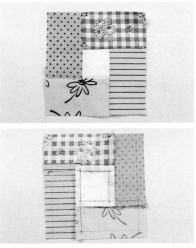

7. Repeat, joining piece E to A/D as shown. Press the seam allowance toward piece E.

8. Fold pieces A, E, and B, which we only sewed halfway. Flip it so that the backs of all three of them face you. Make their marks align and place marking pins on them. Now, backstitch one stitch from the place you stopped before, and continue.

9. Once you sew to the edge, backstitch, and make a French knot. Make the seam allowance rest on the side of piece B. It's finished!

Sewing Curved Lines
How to sew convex and concave lines.

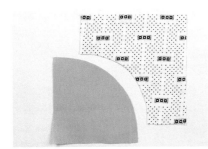

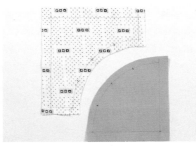

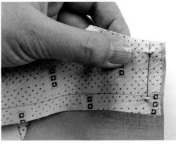

1. Cut the pieces.

2. Make three marks on the back of the curved section. Then, place marking pins from mark to mark and sew in small stitches.

3. Right sides together, place the curved edges of both pieces so raw edges are aligned. Pin to align the edges of both curves in as straight a line as possible.

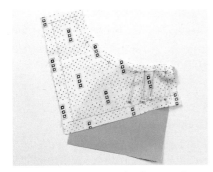

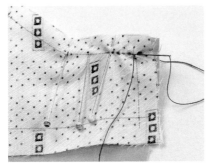

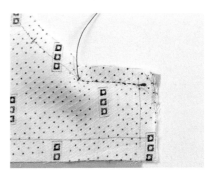

4. Line up and pin at the first marks from step 2. Add pins before and after the mark.

5. Backstitch from the edge and then begin sewing. It's a short distance to the next mark, so it's essentially the same as sewing a straight line.

6. Once you reach the mark, remove the needle temporarily and let it rest.

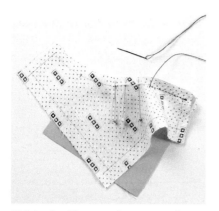

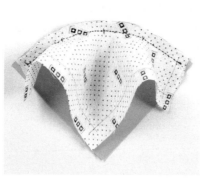

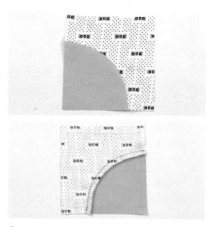

7. Join the fabrics at the next mark, insert pins as we did before, and continue sewing.

8. Repeat this process until you reach the edge of the fabric.

9. Straighten it with an iron and make the seam allowance rest on the convex side of the curve. It's finished.

How to Sew a Circle-Piece Appliqué

We'll place a circle over the main fabric and blindstitch it into place. I'll teach you two methods for making a nice-looking circle.

1. Prepare your base material and your appliqué circle.

2. Sew a running stitch all around the margin of the appliqué circle. Finally, sew the last stitch over the first one.

3. Add a pattern paper of the same size as the stitched circle to the reverse, and pull on the thread to tighten it.

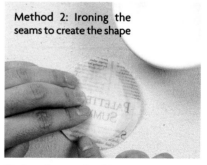

4. Once it's tight, make a French knot and cut the thread. Press it firmly to keep the shape in place. You'll iron both the front and the back side.

5. Take the pattern paper out. You've created an appliqué circle!

6. Another method is to create a water glue by mixing some liquid laundry soap and water at a 1:1 ratio. Add pattern paper to the back of the appliqué circle, and apply water glue to the seam allowance.

7. Use the iron's tip to cause the seam allowance to rise. Use the edges of the pattern paper to make sure you only iron over the allowance.

8. Now the whole seam allowance is flattened down. Since you applied water glue, it will have created a firm and neat circle. You can now remove the pattern paper.

9. Mark with dots at the top, bottom, left, and right indicators of where you'd like your appliqué piece to rest.

10. Place the appliqué piece over those marks, and hold it down with pins.

11. Blindstitch the piece from behind the main material to make the seam invisible. Insert the needle at the top side of the circle's edge, then continue inserting it into the material behind.

12. Blindstitch it around once, and you're done. If you're stitching it in the normal way, use a thread of the same color as the appliqué piece.

How to Sew an Appliqué Stem

We'll create an appliqué that is useful for the thin stem of a plant, or other such shapes, by using bias tape.

1. Create the bias tape. Place a ruler at a 45-degree angle relative to the fabric, and use a rotary cutter to cut a piece with a width of about 1" (2.5cm).

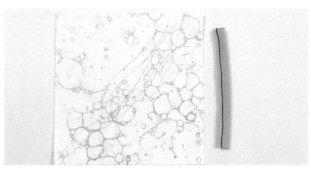

2. Fold the inner and outer sides of the bias tape together and stitch it into a tubular shape with a seam allowance of ³⁄₁₆" (0.5cm). Prepare the base material and make marks where you want the appliqué shape to be placed.

3. Cut the fabric used for the stem to leave a ¹⁄₁₆" (0.2cm) seam allowance, and press it open. Make sure this seam allowance doesn't stick out when seen from the front. Prepare some pattern paper for the stem.

4. Insert the pattern paper into the stem fabric.

5. Once the pattern paper is inside, you'll use an iron to give it shape. Make sure to iron it firmly.

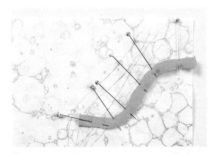

6. Remove the pattern paper and place the piece over the marks made on the base material, holding them down with pins. You gave the piece a curved shape in step 5, so it's now easier to make it match those marks.

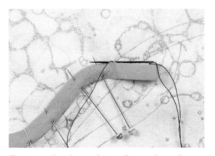

7. Begin backstitching from the edge. Backstitch the opposite side, too.

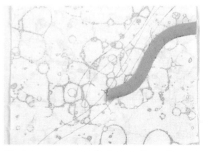

8. Cut any unneeded extra length. It's finished!

How to Flatten a Seam Allowance

It is standard practice to flatten the seam allowance toward the side of the piece that you want to highlight, or toward the side with the pattern shapes on it. Depending on the fabric's thickness or its color, it may be OK to simply flatten it in the direction that is the easiest to flatten.

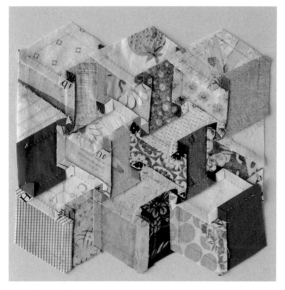

Page 88 Baby's Block

Page 142 Wonder of the World

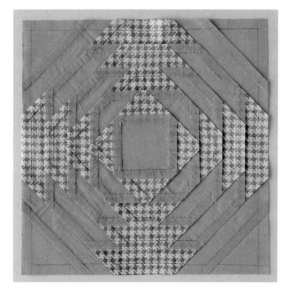

Page 98 Pineapple

Page 125 The Lover's Chain

Tips and Tricks: Choosing Colors and Fabric Designs

When doing patchwork, there will be colors and fabric designs you will find yourself naturally more drawn to use. By learning your own preferred choices, you can begin to make quilts that are more uniquely yours. I'll share mine, and I hope you also think deeply of what choices of color and fabric you tend to make.

Colors I Like

I essentially love all colors, but my base choices are always red, blue, and green. When I say red, I mean most colors ranging from yellowish tones to the deepest crimson. Depending on the tone of red, my desired effect will work or not.

Red. Starting from the left, we have hues that approach deep red, cardinal red, carmine, and Turkey red. Depending on the fabric design, these tones will create one impression or another.

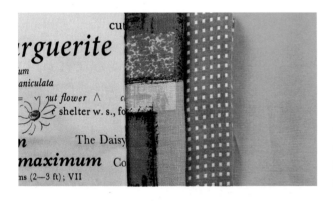

Green. Starting from the left, we have tones close to chartreuse, apple green, forest green, and sea green; what most people consider green to look like. I also like deeper and cooler greens.

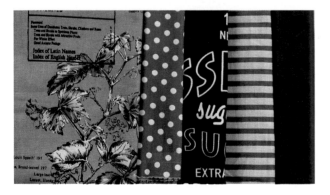

Blue. Starting from the left, we have tones that resemble Saxe blue, with its mix of green and gray, salvia blue, navy, marine blue, and royal blue. Deep blue tones that are closer to black, which are greenish or purplish, are also really fantastic.

Fabric Designs I Like

I like plain fabrics, but choosing between designs is one of the pleasures of patchwork. Occasionally I choose designs based on what they mean or symbolize, but I often do it simply from a design-oriented perspective.

Large Designs. Some may think large designs are hard to use, but they allow the priceless gift of being used in parts. Using just one part of a design gives it a certain movement, and if you cut out an undecorated section of the design, you can use it as a plain color, too. And of course, you can use a large design in its entirety if you're making a large piece.

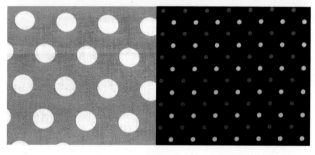

Polka Dots. With dots, the width of the dots and the space between them is key. That will determine whether it looks modern or whether it can almost be used as a plain color. When you examine it closely, the black fabric on the right has a design depicting *konpeito*, a typical Japanese candy.

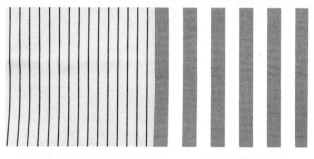

Stripes. The stripes' width and the space between them (their pitch) is essential here. The impression they give changes if they're vertical or horizontal. There are countless combinations of color and pitch possible.

English Print. A fabric design I practically always use is English print. Sometimes I play with the possibility of reading the words, but I generally use these designs in sliced up formats where you can't distinguish the text. The font type, size, and width can greatly determine what impression it gives, so I usually settle on an idea first and find a fabric that works with it.

Tips and Tricks: Choosing Materials and Inspiration

Cotton is very widely used in patchwork quilts, but you can really use any material you like. Also, we're surrounded by wonderful designs and colors in our daily lives but may have taken no note of them. It's important to always try and take an interest in the things that we see.

Materials

Just by choosing a material of a different texture, the depth of the image can change. It can become more charming, too. Still, there are materials that are harder to sew with. Make sure to take care or even adhere some fusible web onto the material.

Lace. Lace is transparent and has holes in it, so we've got to stick some thin, knitted fusible web behind it before using. See page 107 for an example.

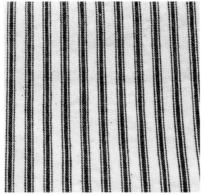

Thick cloth. The picture shows some cloth used for old bed mattresses. This material is so firm that it can't be used for small pieces, but it is great for backgrounds. See page 53 for an example.

Wool. When making winter garments, it looks adorable to use only wool, but personally I tend to combine it with cotton. Be careful because its edges can easily get frayed. See page 139 for an example.

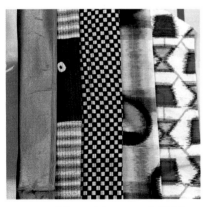

Japanese fabrics. The type of old fabrics used for kimono. A delightful aspect of Japanese fabrics is that they come in many unique colors and designs. They contain a lot of silk, so we use it by sticking thin fusible web behind it. See pages 152 and 153 for examples.

Linen. The photograph shows an old piece of linen with someone's embroidered initials. It's best used for embroidering, as shown on page 121.

Modified fabrics. A fabric with ribbons folded inside it. We can also use fabrics that have never been used before, which are woven in a strange way or are covered in fur, among others. I used velvet in the example on page 133.

Objects I Like

Here are objects I can't use as quilting materials but whose design I like, such as pieces of paper or boxes.

 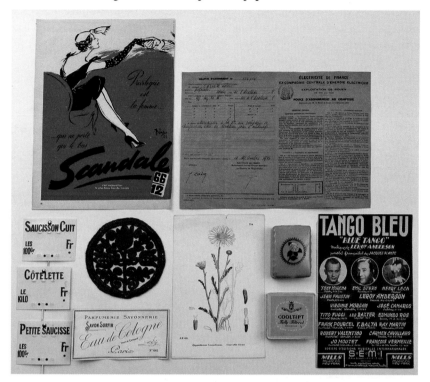

Colorful tape. I adore how the colors are used. It's great inspiration when thinking of combinations.

Posters, order forms, small boxes, postcards. These are finished products that are created by professional designers and put on sale. There's a lot you can learn from them, such as their use of color or the balance of their design.

Tips and Tricks: Choosing and Combining Fabrics

Thinking of ways to combine fabrics and create color combinations is hard but incredibly rewarding. In the case of printed fabrics, one single sheet can include various colors and shapes, so our color combination can vary depending on which section we use.

Combining Two Pieces of Fabric

We'll begin by combining just two sheets of fabric. We must think of how the color, design, and mood of each sheet combine with each other.

Stripes and flower designs. On their own, flower designs look very feminine, but adding stripes stiffens some of that sweetness. Flowers are frequently used on wallpapers in Britain, and they're often combined with stripes.

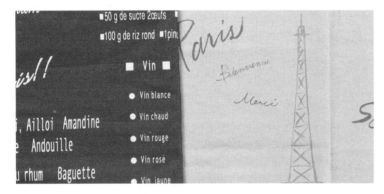

Combining colors contained in the fabric. The intense orange tone on the left can be combined with another orange color. The fabric on the right doesn't contain any orange, but since its pink letters are highlighted by the beige background, they give an impression of being close to orange. It's a fabric combination that allows these intense colors to not look so bare.

Using pink to bring out a mature look. Pink is often seen as a cute color, but combined with black, it becomes much more mature. I recommend combining it with *chidori* designs, a traditional Japanese pattern, to make it look stylish. Or to combine it with stripes to give it a fresh look. This way, it stops being just a cute color and gives off a much more compact aura.

Envisioning Your End Result

When choosing fabrics, it's good to have a clear image of the whole pattern. We must first think about what type of pattern we'd like to make, or what object we'd like to create, and then work to get close to this mental image.

Youthful. Fabric combinations that are fresh, adorable, and filled with energy. Clear, invigorating colors and uncomplicated designs. Here, I've alternated between blue, green, and yellow tones.

Monotone. These are very chic fabric combinations. Even with monotones, the impression given can greatly vary depending on whether the white we use is unbleached or whether it's pure white. That means we can also align different tones of white next to each other.

Vintage and antique. I've only used old materials as examples, but new types of fabric could also be included. On the left, we have a feedsack fabric with English typing on it, and on the right, we have toile de Jouy fabric. They're very different fabrics, one hard and the other elegant, but they're connected by being antique.

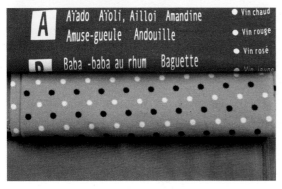

Posters. Color combinations that tend to be used in posters. Despite being simple and using very few colors, they're very impactful. Posters are designed to leave an impression on you even if you just catch a glance, so they're very helpful as an inspiration.

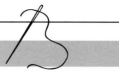

Tips and Tricks: Combining Fabrics in a Pattern

On page 24, we combined various fabrics on their own, but now we'll think of ways to combine them within a pattern.

Combining Fabrics in a Pattern

Even if our fabrics combine on their own, they may create a different impression once we include them in a pattern. It depends on which other pieces it will need to be combined with, what the size and design of these pieces are, and so on. We must try out different types of fabric until we find a color combination that appeals to us. For these examples, I'll use a Basket pattern.

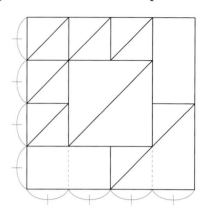

The First Materials We Choose

Green, brown, and other deep and chic tones over a white base with English letters. At this stage, this mix has a very calm hue. Now we can cut them into the sizes necessary for our pattern and see how they look.

We'll use the plain white material as a base, and the yellow and brown colors for those small triangle shapes.

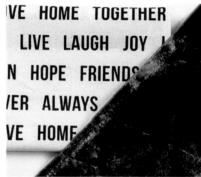

We could use this velvet material or this white fabric with English print for the large triangle in the center.

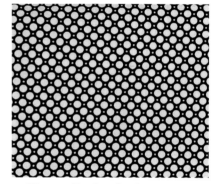

We'll use polka dots for the lower triangle.

Our Next Choice of Material

Our first selection was just one possibility, so here are even more materials.

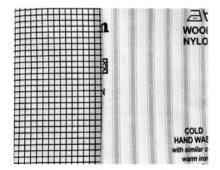

We'll change the base material. Here, I've chosen a checkered fabric and a striped material with English letters. The checkered material might be a little too loud for our uses.

Additional choices for our small triangle pieces. This yellow is too vivid, so maybe the yellow tone we chose before is better.

Here's a large-scale-design fabric for the central triangle. We can use either its plain green parts or its designed parts.

Two Types of Practically Completed Patterns:

The central triangle looks good both in option A and option B. The woven design of option B gives it a very serious look, and this makes the lower polka dot triangles look a bit feeble. Because of that, we can exchange them for the velvet material if we want, as shown in C.

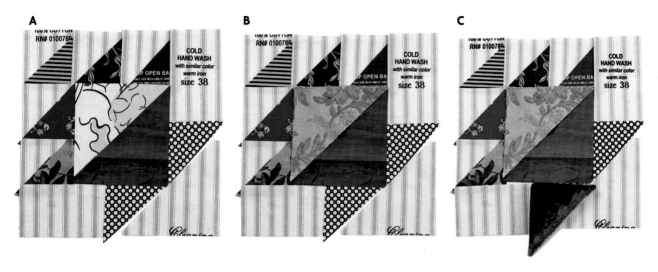

Glossary of Terms

Backing. The back of the quilt.

Batting. The filler between the backing and the quilt top.

Binding. To cover the seam allowance around a quilt and fix it into place using bias tape or other methods.

Block. One of the units that comprises a quilt design, such as a pattern or others.

Border. A belt-shaped fabric placed around the edge of a block.

Drop quilting. A form of quilting where you insert into the edge of a piece or an appliqué seam.

Lattice. A belt-shaped fabric used to connect blocks together.

Piece. The smallest units of fabric used. They are created by drawing the marks from a pattern paper onto fabric and then cutting around those marks.

Piecing. To sew different pieces together.

Quilting. A process of stitching three layers together with small stitches. These layers are the backing, batting, and quilt top, in that same order.

Quilting line. A line on the diagram sheets. The quilting line travels from the top (the front of the fabric) to the backing.

Top. The front side of a quilt. Some are made from piecing, while others are an entire section of cloth.

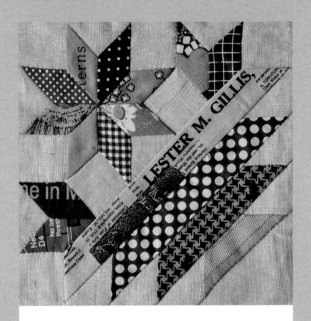

Representational Patterns

Patterns that represent flowers, birds, living beings, or the shape and appearance of certain objects. Many other patterns simply display abstract shapes, so these are uniquely easy to understand and adorable.

Baskets

Patterns shaped like baskets. Many of them are slanted to one side, but some of them are also front-facing or show many baskets in the same image.

Basket I

A soft red is used for the handle, which adds balance to the composition. The fabric used for the basket also has some red designs on it, which links the two parts.

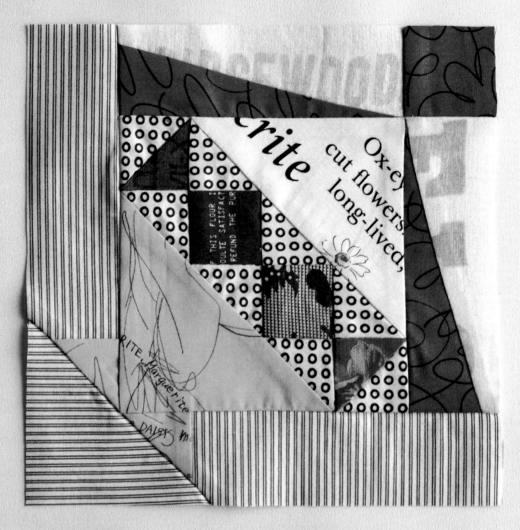

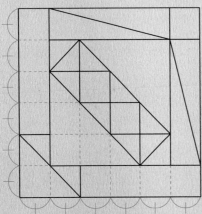

Basket II

A green basket with a blue handle,
a refreshing combination of colors.
A daisy can peek over the basket's
rim, making it seem like it's filled
with flowers.

Friendship Basket

The entire base material has the same rough texture, but the basket itself is made of many different kinds of fabric. It's a great example of how much fun you can have combining materials.

- There is a half-size pattern diagram on page 193.

Use this diagonal line to divide it into a top and bottom section

Drawn at a 1:√2 ratio

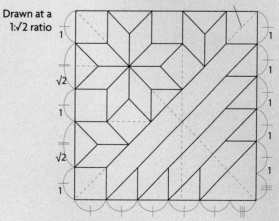

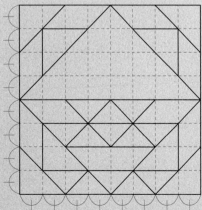

Victorian Basket

Inspired by Victorian-era
decorations, I have used a fabric
design that displays large flowers. A
unified, calm color scheme is used
for the whole pattern.

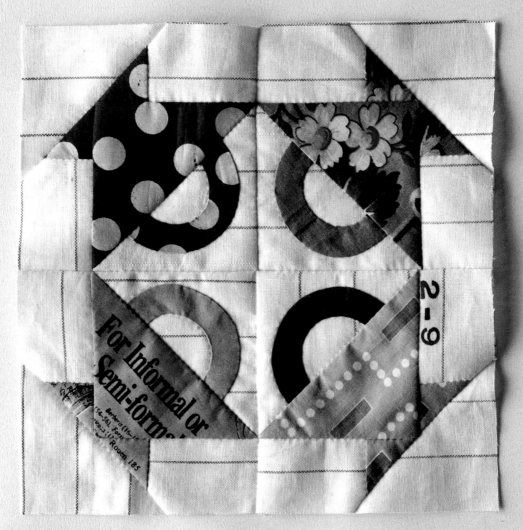

Stamp Basket

This simple and cute pattern was
even used on stamps in the United
States. Each basket uses its own
fabric design to avoid confusion
amongst them. Their handles are an
appliqué of curved pieces of fabric.

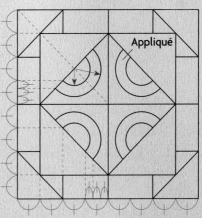

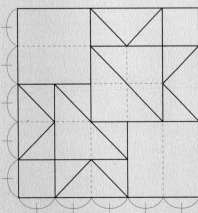

Double Basket

A shape that looks like two baskets joined together. The baskets are all made of entirely different pieces of fabric, but this disparity finds resolution in the vivid orange color used for a base.

Plants

Here are a great number of patterns depicting plants, sometimes the plant as a whole or sometimes just its flowers. You can also find specific flowers in these patterns that you like and can make an entire quilt just for them.

Lily Original

Many quilting patterns depict lilies. Their slightly curved stem and leaves are done by appliqué. Check page 18 for instructions on how to add this appliqué stem.

- There is a half-size pattern diagram on page 193.

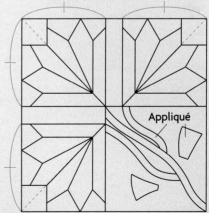

All three flowers are identical, with their centers creating a bilateral symmetry through diagonals

Single Lily

A single lily. Its stem is created by fixing a cord with couching stitches. Its leaves are added by appliqué.

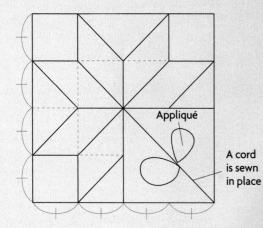

Appliqué

A cord is sewn in place

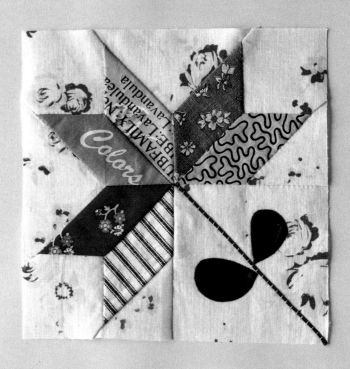

Basket of Lilies

A combination of the flowers and baskets' themes. Their stripes, polka dots, and English print give them a modern look.

- There is a half-size pattern diagram on page 194.

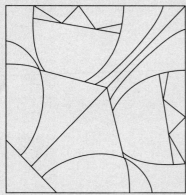

Draw the pattern freely using the diagonal to create bilateral symmetry

Dandelion

I chose a lively yellow base to give
it a dandelion look but chose more
mature fabric designs to avoid it
feeling too childish.

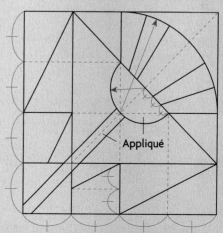

Appliqué

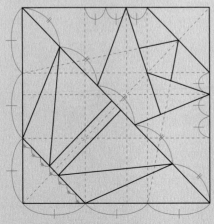

Tulip

Tulips are considered cutesy, but these red, blue, white, and charcoal-gray tones transform it into something more stylish. The stem is made by piecing, not appliqué.

Tassel Plant

The orange and gray parts are a plain, solid color that makes their shapes stand out. The polka-dot base gives it a more Pop Art feel.

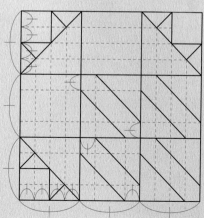

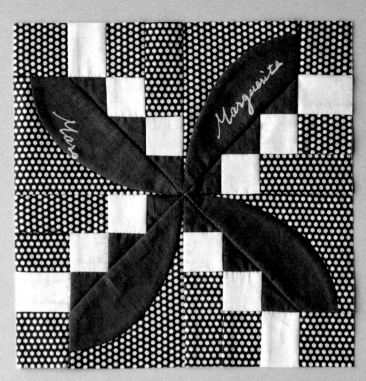

Lily of the Valley

The top example is closer to what a lily of the valley looks like, with green leaves and white flowers. The bottom example uses a softer color combination.

These curved shapes are drawn by hand

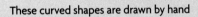

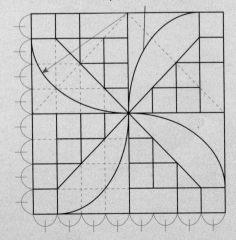

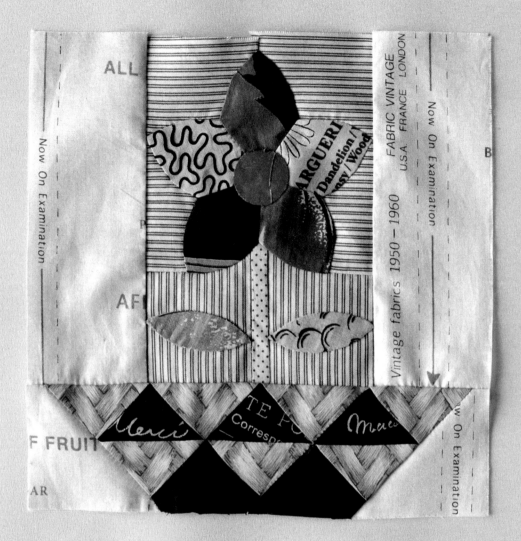

Arkansas
Meadow Rose

A simple and uncomplicated pattern. The leaves, stem, and center of the flower are appliqué, the petals themselves having been pieced together.

- There is a half-size pattern diagram on page 194.

For the flower, choose a size that fits the overall balance

The Flower Pot Quilt

A simple pattern that represents a flower in a flowerpot by piecing squares together.

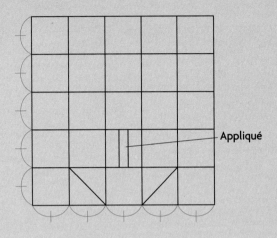

Appliqué

Rose

These triangles help envisage the overlapping petals of a rose. Only the center piece is a square, the rest being triangles of different sizes, sewn in a circling motion around it.

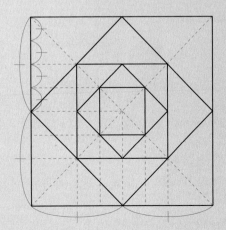

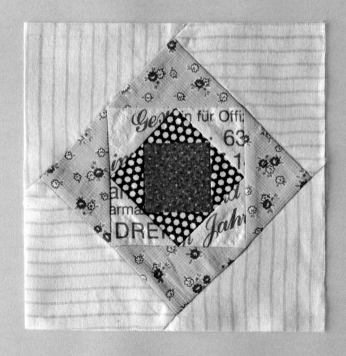

Avalanche Lily

Avalanche lily is the English name for Erythronium montanum, a member of the Liliaceae family. Its large petals are sewn by piecing. It's a very striking pattern.

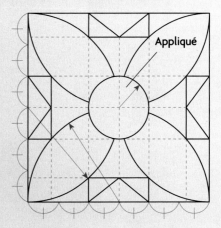

Appliqué

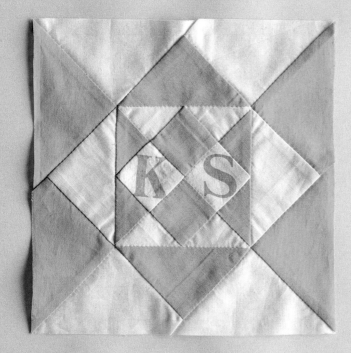

Cockscomb

Even as a patchwork pattern, the cockscomb flower looks like a chicken's crest. Instead of red, I chose simple green and white tones.

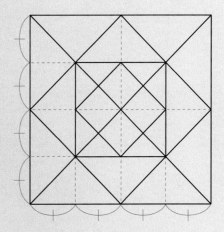

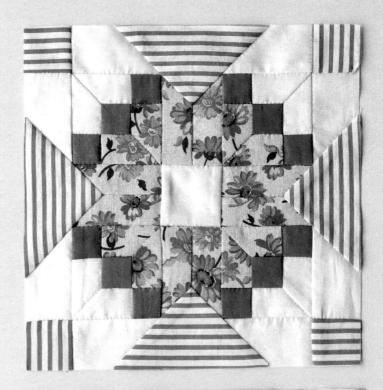

Old-Fashioned Daisy

The fabric used on both examples is the same, but the top one has prominent white petals, a typical feature of daisies.

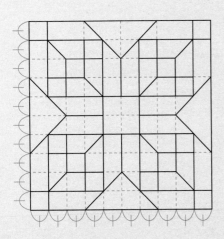

Magnolia Blossom

A pattern that depicts a flower as if seen from above. It includes a lot of curves and appliqué work, making it a difficult pattern both to diagram and to sew.

- There is a half-size pattern diagram on page 195.

Extend a line from the center of the main circle, and use it as a pivot to draw circles of any size you wish

The circle can be any size you want

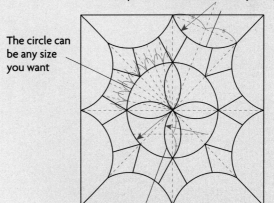

Use the extended lines as a pivot to draw these circles, with their size relative to the main circle

Four-Leaf Clover

It is said its four leaves symbolize hope, sincerity, love, and good luck. It looks good either when made with fabrics of different types or as a coherent striped design, like the top example shows.

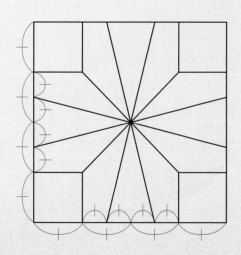

Irish Spring

This shows a budding leaf in spring. It uses bold fabric designs together with a youthful green tone.

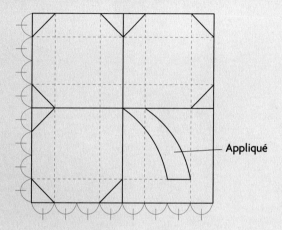

Appliqué

Autumn Leaves

Fallen leaves in tones of yellow, red, and brown, and a pattern that makes them look like they're still fluttering down.

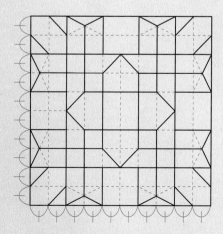

Trail of the Lonesome Pine

Out of these three sections of sloping leaves, only the top canopy has a darker tone. This gives the whole block a good balance.

Draw the curved lines by hand

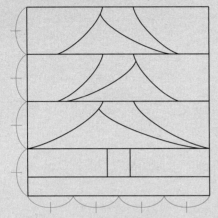

Mushrooms

Four mushrooms. They're all the same block shape but faced in different directions. However, they really give the appearance of being a group of cute little mushrooms.

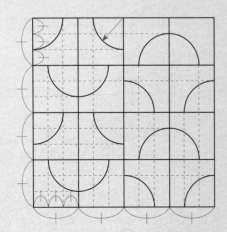

Animals

These patterns not only try to emulate the shapes of various animals, but also some of them try to symbolize animals through more abstract ways. Essentially, this section gathers patterns with animal names in the title.

Calico Cat

This pattern looks like four cats playing together. You could embroider their faces, too, to make them cuter. Once their faces have been sewn on, you can sew them all around the central square.

Sew them around

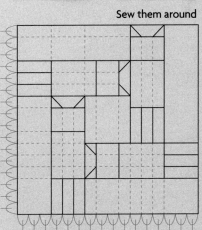

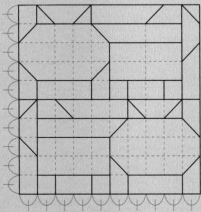

Cats

This Cat pattern shows two of them. They're walking with their tails held high. I have used English-print designs for both of their fabrics, unifying their look. However, their print designs have different sized fonts, keeping them individual.

Georgia's Owl

I chose brown-toned fabrics to make it resemble an owl. This pattern keeps one eye shut to make it seem like it's sleeping, but you can sew the eyes in any style.

- There is a half-size pattern diagram on page 195.

Appliqué

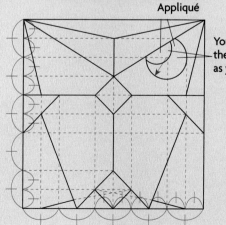

You can make the eye as big as you like

Jonathan Livingston Seagull

A pattern that depicts a seagull flying in the air, inspired by the novel *Jonathan Livingston Seagull*. The top example uses white fabric to resemble a real seagull. The bottom example, however, uses a patterned fabric that makes it look more like an airplane.

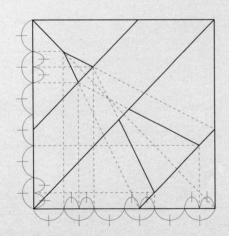

The Big Chicken

A chicken that just radiates charm. Its stark design, with plain cloth, stripes, and polka dots also helps make it look more cheerful.

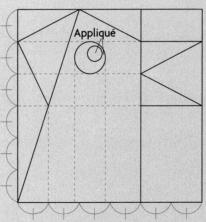

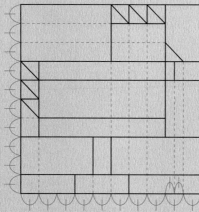

Hen

A pattern that depicts a chicken, like on page 53, but this time its whole body. Switching the direction of the stripes helps differentiate between her head and wings.

Dove in the Window

I have used two simple, plain colors to create this image. Just like the pattern on page 170, this one can be split around the central point.

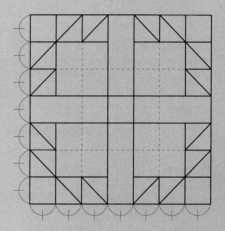

Fox and Geese

Fox and Geese is the name of a board game. Like that game, this pattern exudes the excitement of not knowing whether the fox will trap the geese or the geese will chase down the fox.

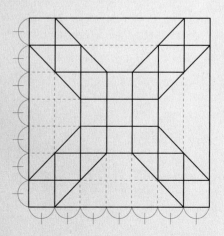

Wild Goose Chase

This phrase signals pursuits that are futile, since geese are very hard to catch. There's another quilting pattern with this name that joins crosses and straight lines.

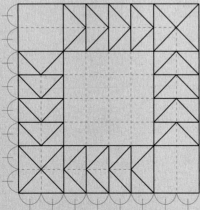

Turtle I

A pattern that shows cute, little turtles. To enhance these Turtle patterns, I've combined them with two other plain squares, but you can also keep the turtle sections independent.

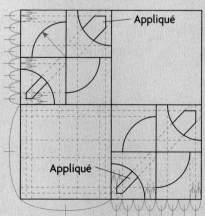

Appliqué

Appliqué

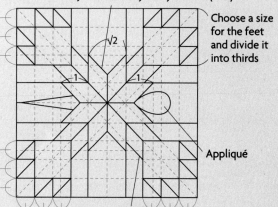

Draw a LeMoyne Star at any size you wish (1:√2)

Choose a size for the feet and divide it into thirds

√2

1 1

Appliqué

This section should connect with one of the thirds of the feet

Turtle II

Here is a very dynamic pattern of a turtle. Its central section, the turtle's shell, is a LeMoyne Star, a well-known shape in patchwork art.

• There is a half-size pattern diagram on page 196.

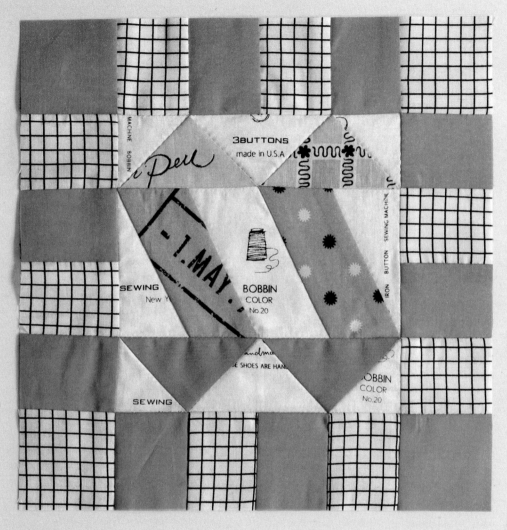

Cobra

Even such dangerous creatures as cobras become cute when sewn as patterns. The combination of gold and white gives it a Pop Art feel.

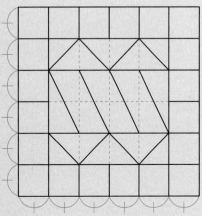

Stars

Stars are known as a popular type of pattern, but in fact, there are many different kinds of stars. It's important to get their edges looking nice and sharp.

Cluster of Stars

A pattern depicting several stars together. Just as different stars shine with different lights, the use of varied fabrics helps to keep them individual.

Shooting Star I

This pattern is sewn around a central square. I have chosen black and mint blue to evoke cosmic space.

Sew around the center

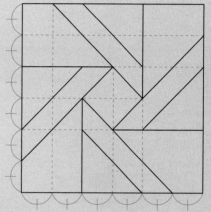

Shooting Star II

This shooting star has a more visually striking tail, so it looks to be moving at great speed. To achieve this, I've used somewhat loud colors.

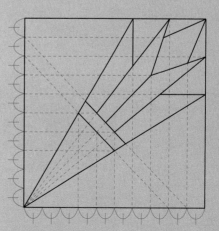

Twin Stars

A couple of twin stars. The top example is decorated entirely with dots of different sizes. The bottom example is more unique, even using leopard print.

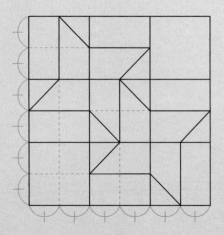

Natchez Star

Natchez is a city in the United States. Its shape is simple, but the striped design gives it a sense of movement.

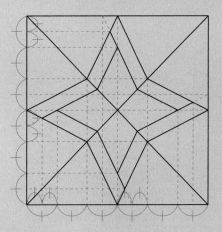

Texas Star I

Here we have the name of another location in the United States: Texas. The asymmetry in this star shape makes it a very interesting pattern. The star section is composed of completely different pieces of fabric.

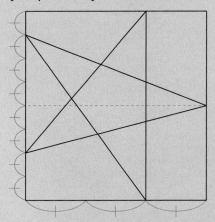

The Old Stars and Stripes

Aligning the direction of the English print and the stripes gives a very complex appearance to these blocks. The Stars and Stripes refers to the flag of the United States.

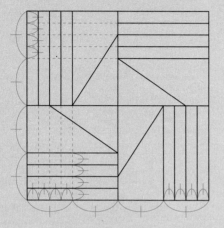

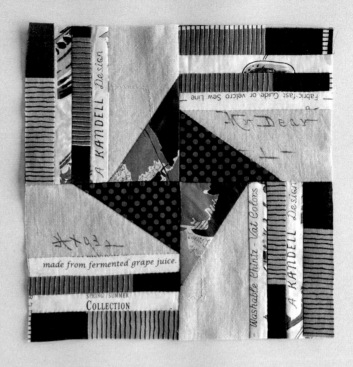

Star of Zamberland

It's an overall manly color combination, but the key design choice was to make the central square charcoal gray instead of black to avoid it becoming too strong of a composition.

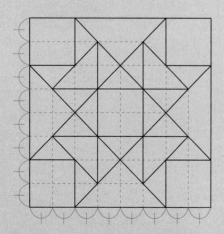

Wisconsin Star

Since this is a hexagonal star, it can only be sewn into a hexagon, like in the bottom example. The top example combines similarly toned fabrics for a gentle mood. The bottom one strikes a balance between different colors.

- There is a half-size pattern diagram on page 196.

Draw a hexagon and unite its different points, using your measurements of choice

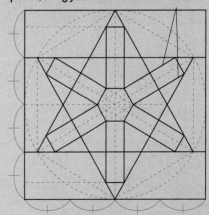

After drawing the surrounding hexagon, you can calculate the size of the inner hexagons

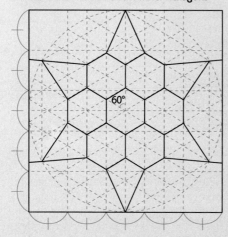

Grandmother's Star

This wonderful pattern uses the classic Grandmother's Flower Garden pattern, a union of hexagons, as a central element. It involves plenty of inlay sewing.

- There is a half-size pattern diagram on page 197.

Framed Star

The star is made of red and light green plain cloth, with the rest being made of gray print fabrics. This creates a color scheme that highlights the star.

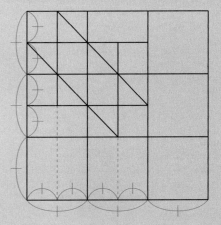

Stacked Stars

A pattern that locks the star's pointed edges into each other, like a puzzle. I took care to create the tone scheme, keeping in mind the differences in color and fabric design between stars.

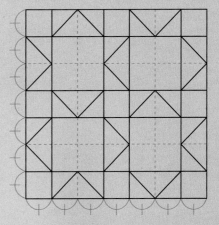

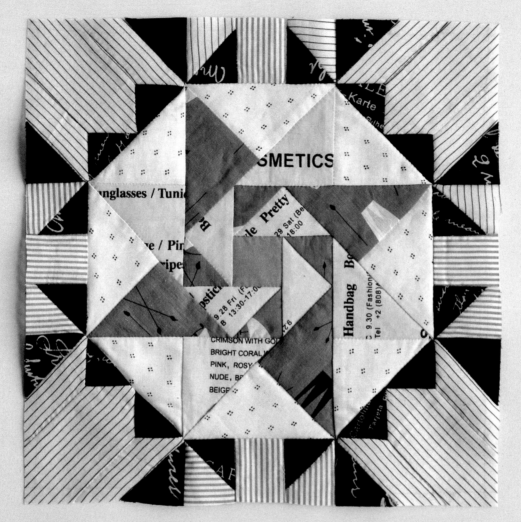

The main octagon needs to be
sewn around the center

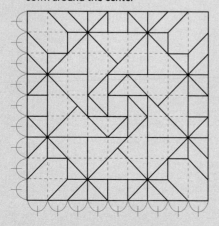

Unfolding Star

It's a complicated shape with a
lot of pieces, so I created it in
9½" x 9½" (24 x 24cm). It makes the
central star, and its surrounding
triangles stand out. The central
section requires you to sew around
the square, so it's a slightly more
complex procedure.

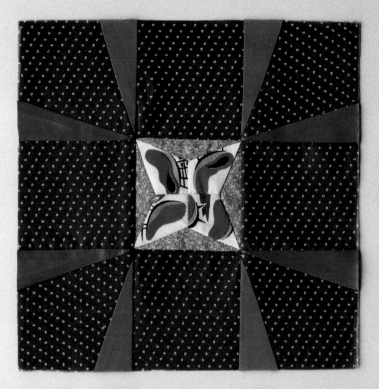

Star Chain

No matter how many versions of this pattern I sew, the stars always end up tied up, like a spider web. In both cases, I have chosen a mix of vivid colors and cooler tones.

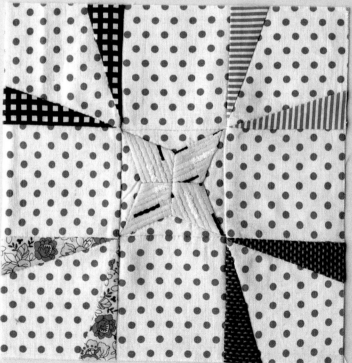

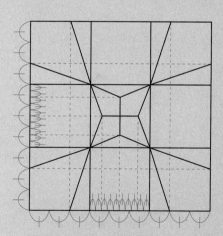

Crosses

Patterns that are shaped like crosses. There also are many more patterns with names based on crosses and on saints.

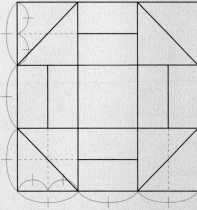

Greek Cross

The key feature of a Greek Cross is that it intersects at the center. Some patterns orient it diagonally. To avoid it looking too heavy, I've used pink colors.

Cross and Crown I

The cross and crown is a traditional Christian symbol. It is often used as a pattern in different shapes.

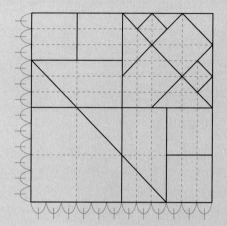

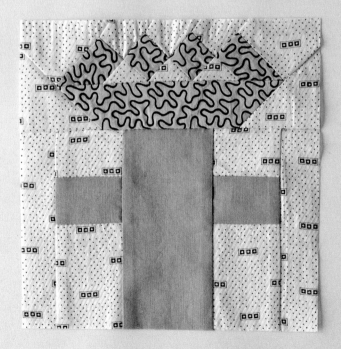

Cross and Crown II

A crown on top of a cross; a unique design almost resembling a growing plant. It's simple, but its combination of gold and sky blue catches the eye.

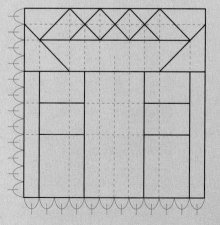

Schoenrock Cross

I used green tones on both examples, but the top one feels more autumnal whereas the bottom example feels lighter, more reminiscent of spring.

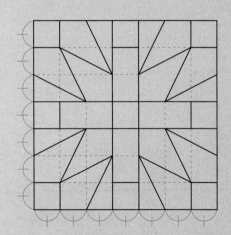

Christian Cross

Even if just using mint and white, the pattern's shape is clearly discernible. The fabric designs help distinguish the different parts.

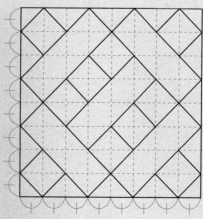

Houses

Some have chimneys and windows, and some have a little path that leads up to the front door. There are many patterns of houses, all of them cute and very recognizable.

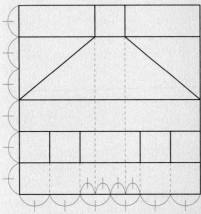

House I

A house with a very simple shape. I chose these fabrics to evoke a house in a bright, rural area surrounded by many plants.

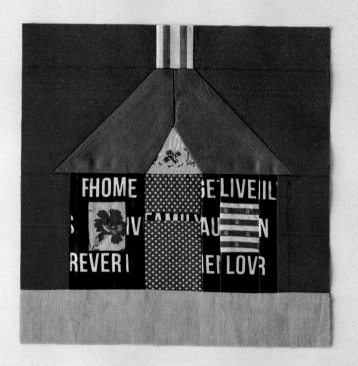

House II

I chose a very vivid shade of red for the background, and it had the counterintuitive effect of making the house stand out. The windows let you see the same color being used again on its red designs.

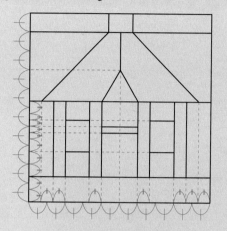

House III

I used a big fabric design that really stands out for the roof piece, making it look like an abstract painting. Considering what type of home you'd like to create is a fun aspect of quilting houses.

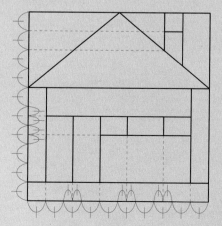

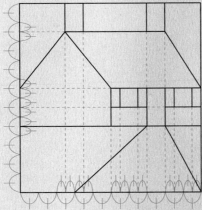

House IV

A quilted house I could almost call
a staple of mine. The little path is
next to a field of grass and a flower
bed, represented by a fabric with
a flower design. The front door
and windows are very bright.
Even the windowless sections use
a latticework-print fabric, which
evokes the shapes of windows.

Other Patterns

All other kinds of representational patterns.

Airplane

I chose a color combination that makes it look cute and retro, like a toy airplane. With the English-print design, it calls to mind something from the United States of old.

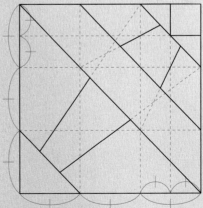

Spool I

On the latticework sections, I playfully added designs of fashion items slightly related to threading and spools. On the other hand, I kept the color scheme simple and light with gold and blue.

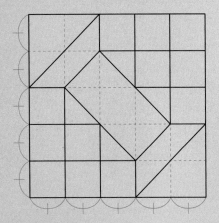

Spool II

They're all the same Spool pattern, but when multiplied by four, it becomes even cuter. We could also change the direction they're facing.

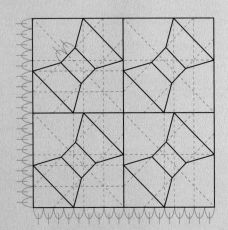

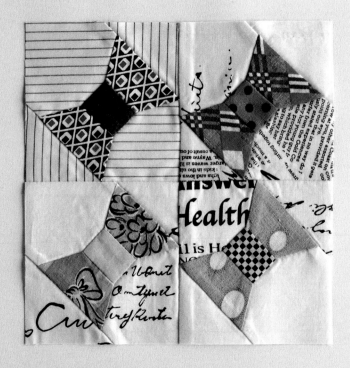

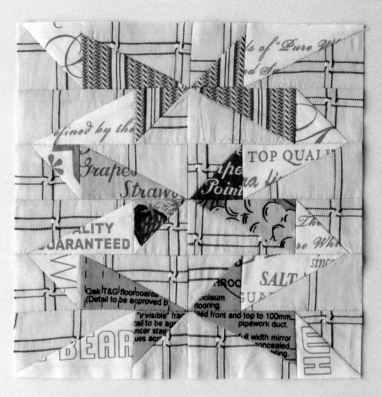

Bowknots

Both examples are the same, but the tips of the bowknots use different cloths. Just by making the tips a deep or a light color, the picture changes.

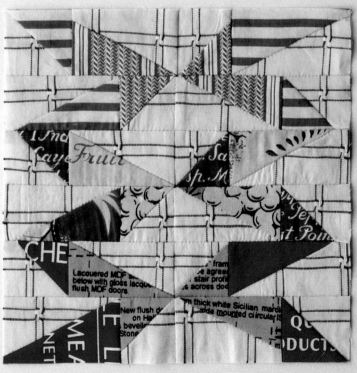

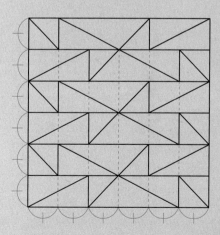

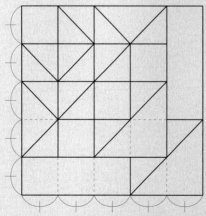

Cake Stand

The colors of this cake stand give it a serious, mature look. Charcoal gray for the base and an assortment of chic colors for the inner pattern give the mature tones a cuter look.

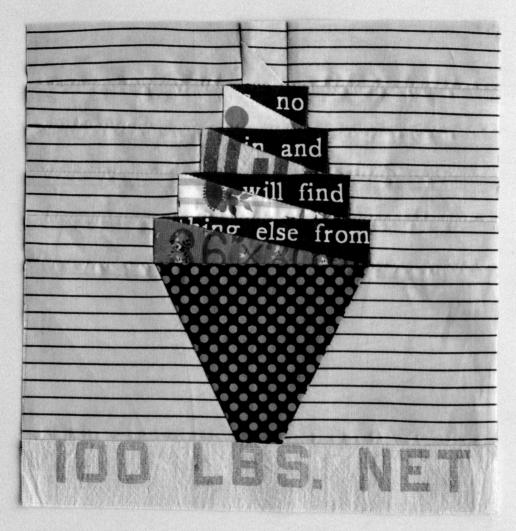

Soft Serve Ice Cream Original

It's a simple image of an ice cream with a cute color combination of pink and light blue. A fun aspect of this pattern is choosing what fabric designs you'll use for the ice cream part.

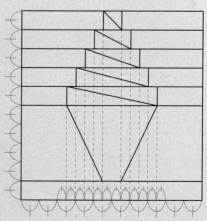

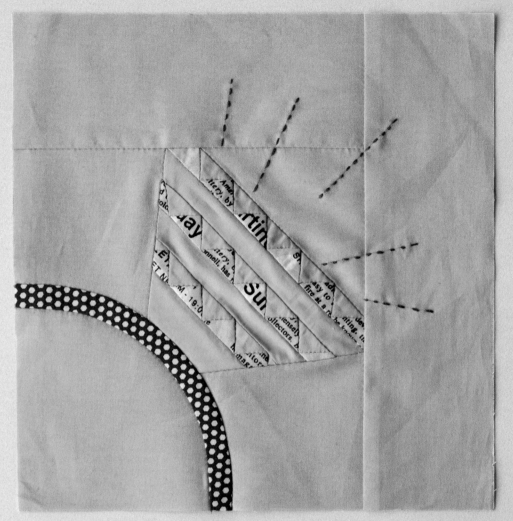

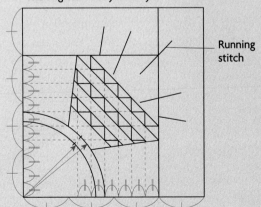

The ring can be any width you want

Running stitch

Diamond Original

A pattern that depicts a diamond ring. The lines that represent sparkle are embroidered with a running stitch. The diamond is made from very small pieces, so make sure to cut the edges just right.

Wedding Ring

A mix of blue and yellow; two colors that fit together well. By using a flower design, I gave it a brighter, more exuberant look.

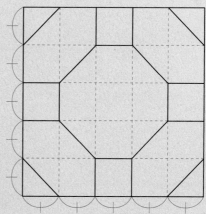

Anvil

An anvil is a workbench used to craft metal objects. This use of black and white stripes and fabric designs with black portions gives it a firm look.

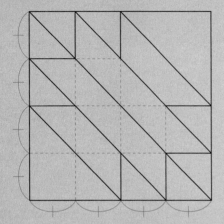

Honeycomb

A Honeycomb pattern. It allows for a great number of variations. Since it's such a simple piece, it's fun to use a fabric with large designs on it.

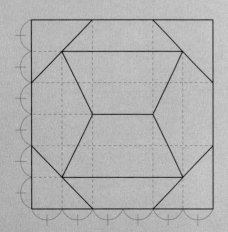

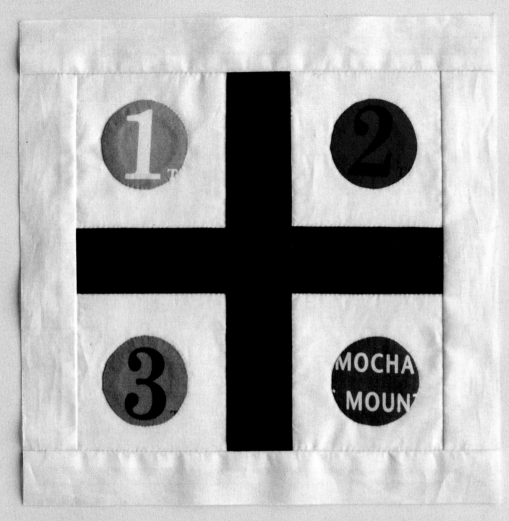

The Kanji for "Rice"

This pattern is based on the Japanese character for rice. A pattern that is minimalist, modern, and uniquely Japanese.

The size and position of the appliqué can be varied

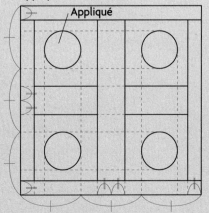

Color Step Original

The contrast between the plain tones and the white sections really highlights the colors. I chose English print that matches the plain-colored parts to add a sense of rhythm.

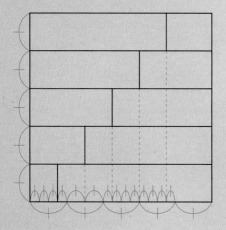

Window

A pattern that's slanted diagonally. It's fun to imagine what's inside the window and what's outside, and to choose fabrics accordingly.

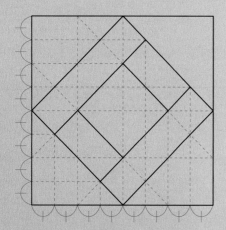

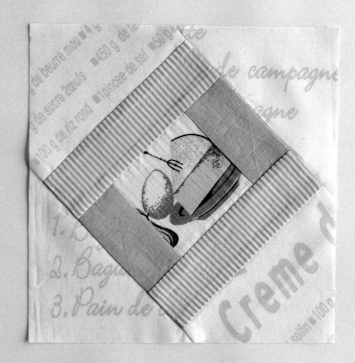

Patterns Divided
by Shape

Some of them are triangular V designs. In
some, the main focus are diagonally placed
X marks. I've tried dividing these patterns
by these distinctive features, and some I have
divided by their overall shape.

One-Patch Patterns

One-Patch Patterns are patterns made from chaining together several shapes, be they rhombi, hexagons, etc. They're repetitions of the same shape, so their color schemes become much more important.

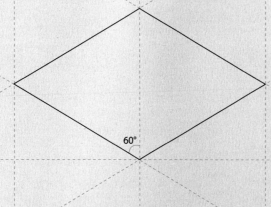

This diagram shows the actual 1:1 piece size

60°

Baby's Block

By combining rhombus pieces with three color tones—light, half-dark, and dark (all with designs on them)—I can create a box shape. This is easier if you arrange your fabrics by shade and then create a color scheme. Sew the pieces within the design section, and leave some margin to pinwheel your seams.

Cotton Reel

I created squares out of four triangle pieces. Combining the darker and lighter shades makes the pattern really stand out. By alternating the lighter hues of color, you add variety to the mix.

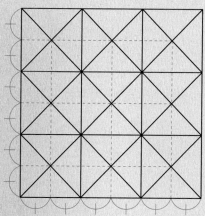

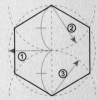

This diagram shows the actual 1:1 piece size

Compote of Flowers

A pattern where a vase of flowers is drawn with only hexagons. Just like in a coloring book, I've used different tones for the background, flowers, and vase. I first sewed hexagons into single rows and sewed all those horizontal rows together.

Diamond Field

Each diamond is composed of
nine hexagons. If you surround the
diamond's center with six hexagons
instead, you'd create a pattern called
Grandmother's Flower Garden.

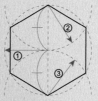

This diagram shows the actual 1:1 piece size

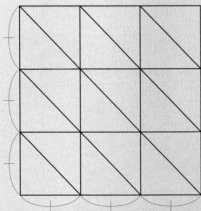

Mosaic

A pattern made of connected triangles. I sewed each pair of triangles into a square block, with one triangle being a light shade and the other a dark shade.

Tumbler

A tumbler is a large-scale cup.
Try first envisioning a series of
multicolored tumblers, and sew
them into reality.

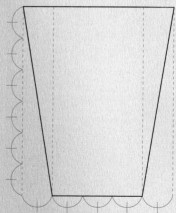

Log Cabin Series

These are patterns where rectangular or trapezium shapes are increasingly stacked one on top of the other. Something that's interesting about them is that their pattern name can change depending on the color combination used.

Courthouse Steps

On each side of the central squares, rectangles of the same length are sewn alternatingly. They look like staircases of four steps, extending in four directions from the center. When neighboring pieces collide, they create a shape like a rhombus, which gives this pattern an extra charm.

Log Cabin I

Here, the rectangles are sewn in a spiraling motion around the central square. For the color scheme, I used the central diagonal line to divide the pattern into light and dark areas.

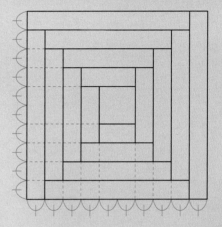

Log Cabin II

Like above, here rectangles are sewn in a spiraling motion around the central square. However, the width of the square and the rectangles is the same.

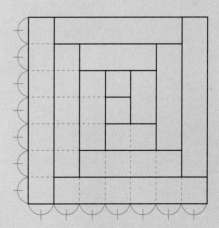

95

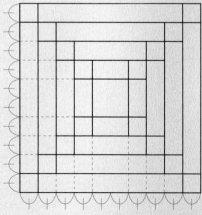

Chimney and Cornerstones I

As you connect the pieces of this pattern, diagonal white grid lines appear. When the lines become connected to the neighboring pieces, they add a sense of coherence to the picture.

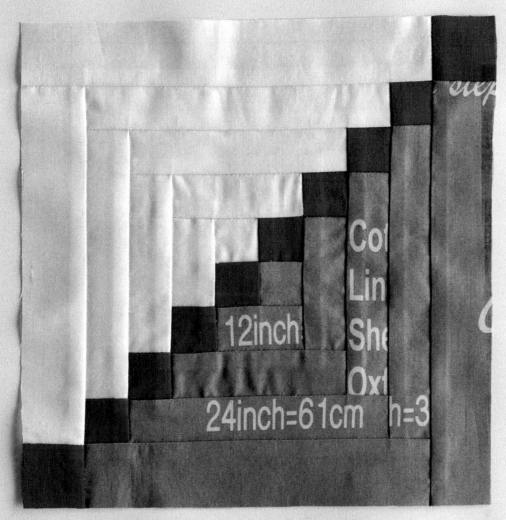

Chimney and Cornerstones II

This is also the Chimney and Cornerstones pattern. You can sew these patterns many times, and depending on how you orient the direction of the pieces, the entire design can change.

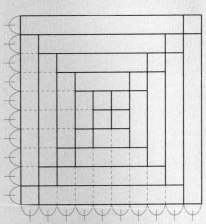

Pineapple

A fun pattern that consists of serrated edges expanding outward. The color balance is obtained by combining plain gold fabric and a fabric with a houndstooth pattern, known as *chidori* in Japan.

Patterns with Triangles

A collection of patterns that include a lot of triangular pieces, or where triangles are a characteristic feature. Triangular pieces always have a bias direction that makes them stretch, so be careful not to pull on them while sewing.

Cut-Glass Dish

As the name evokes, this pattern is inspired by a sparkling dish made by cut-glass technique. I used a somewhat elegant combination of fabrics.

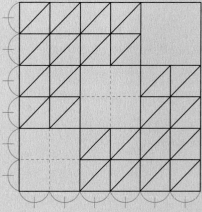

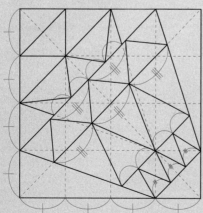

Ice Cream Bowl

I used blue and white as a base
to make it feel cool. It's more of a
mature ice cream bowl.

Ships A-Sailing

It seems to be representing ship sails and waves. I used a gray and white grid to unify the image stylishly. As a base, I used a fabric whose design seems to depict paper mail.

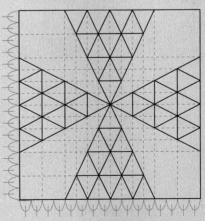

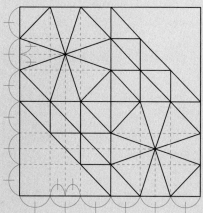

Industrial Age

I used deep green to give it a calm color combination. It's the fabric with a large green pattern, which I introduced on page 21. It serves as an example of how both plain-color and design sections can be seen depending on how you cut the fabric.

Memory Blocks

The central cross and the surrounding triangles in this pattern are visually striking. Make sure to avoid facing the stripes in different directions when aligning them.

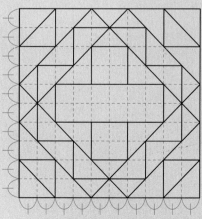

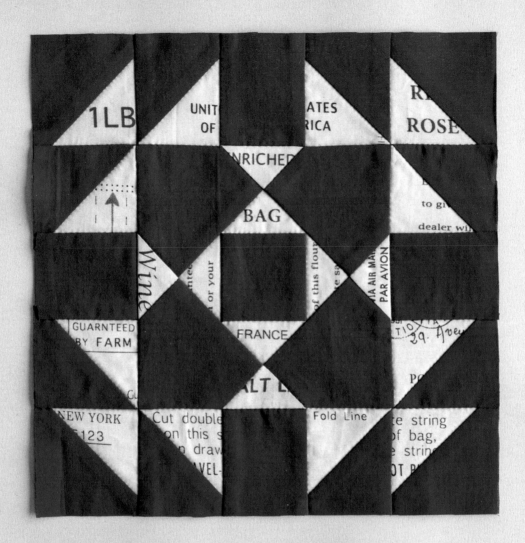

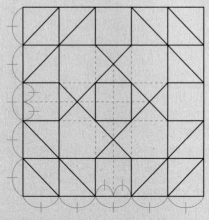

Handy Andy

Red and white is a charming color combination, but that doesn't mean it isn't striking. It's important to spread around the English print in the white triangles as if you're peeking through a hole.

Courthouse

Courthouse is a solemn name for a
pattern, but by using a cute fabric
design, it acquires an antique look.

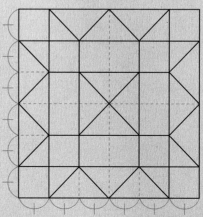

A Focus on Diagonal Lines

Patterns where diagonal lines always cross the center of the image. Some consist of a square that has been cut up into diagonal sections and those blocks are then rotated around, or some consist of slanted rectangle blocks sewn together.

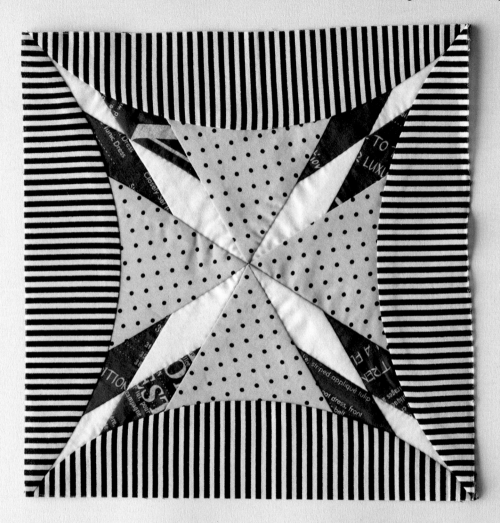

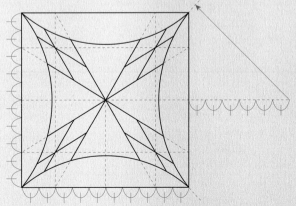

Arabic Tent

A pattern that consists of thin lines that extend toward the corners of the image, and curved lines that give a sense of movement to the whole. Black stripes give it a sharp and modern look.

Jack's Blocks

A pattern where a central square extends outward toward the corners, giving it a sense of stability. I used lace to avoid it being overpowered by the intense red and distinctive black.

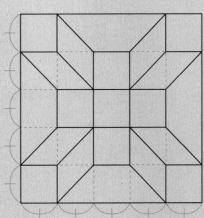

Chevrons

A simple but charming pattern that takes a striped mountain-shaped block and rotates it around. I tried using many different scraps of material.

Twin Darts

I think of it as triangular blocks divided into diagonals. They look like arrows next to their negative image, designed in red and checkerboard.

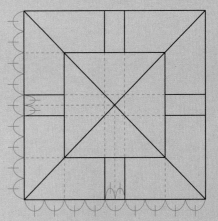

Washington's Puzzle

This pattern looks like nine connected squares tilted to the side. I added striped designs to add intensity to some of its feminine look. I tried to keep the striped patterns aligned.

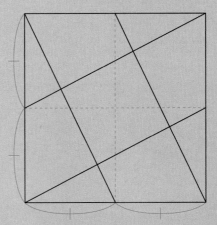

Four Points

Pale yellow and grey make a great mix.
Adding a gingham pattern to the surrounding
areas gives it a fresh look.

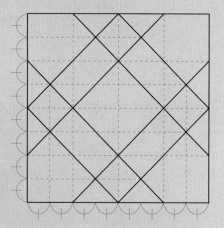

Jacks

Diagonally tilted squares that are further
divided into triangles, all sewn together. The
color scheme can change depending on which
parts you want to highlight.

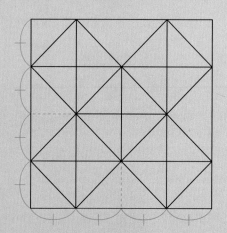

Quilt in Light & Dark

Intersecting blocks that I have given light and dark colors respectively. These are large-sized pieces, so large-size fabric designs are also a wonderful choice.

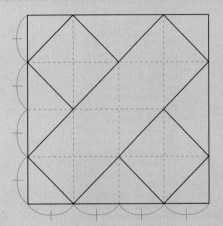

The House Jack Built

It's similar to the pattern on page 110, but in this case, the squares are created by sewing three rectangles together. By using a large-size fabric design as background, the whole becomes more dynamic.

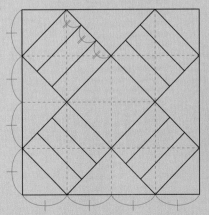

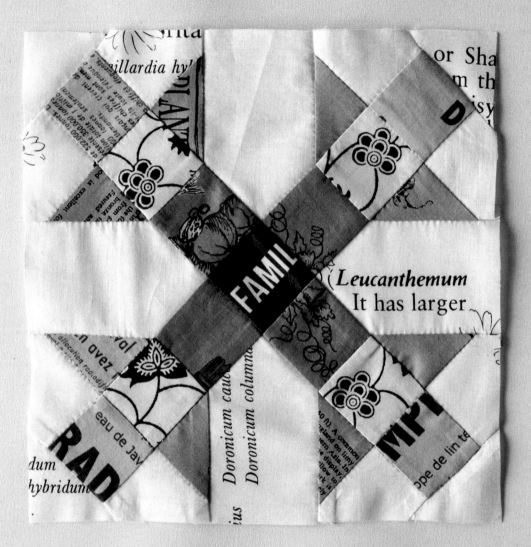

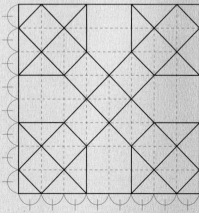

Heather Square

Heather is a plant, in the family
Ericaceae, that is famous in Britain.
This pattern seems to show thin
branches and leaves that bloom
into flowers.

Cross and Square Original

Using a striped design really highlights the central cross, and the alphabet-themed fabrics give it all a modern-design look.

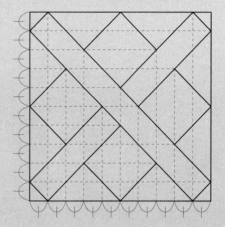

Crossbar

I used red and black on this banded crossbar to make it really stand out. The print used as a base really mellows out these strong colors and gives the pattern a sweeter feeling.

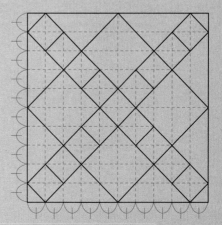

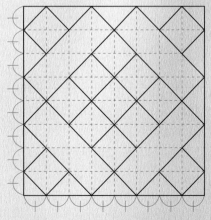

Washington Pavement

An overall pale tone helps to give it a relaxed mood. When adding the print fabric, I gave them all different sizes and fonts.

Bright Side

Black and red make a very intense background combination, but using flower patterns avoids being too overpowering. It's a color scheme that evokes Eastern Europe.

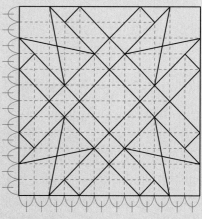

Mandalas

These amusing patterns are sewn together a number of times to create an expanding mandala. They're fun because out of the combination of various pieces emerge entirely new shapes.

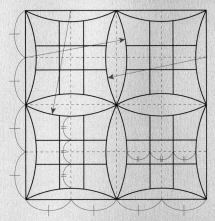

Glorified Nine-Patch

We first sew a Nine Patch pattern and combine it with curved line pieces. I personally like using dark and light colors for the Nine Patch sections.

Hook and Ladder

I alternated the colors of the central triangles to give it a feeling of rhythm. It's fun how the triangles connect to form a line.

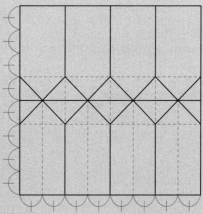

Stick Diamond

I unified the background with a white fabric, which helps make the slanted squares stand out. Apart from this plain white cloth, every other piece uses completely different materials.

The World Fair Quilt

This is composed of only two
types of pieces: oblong hexagons
and slanted squares. I chose to
use leftover material in a scrap-
quilt style.

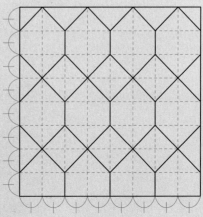

119

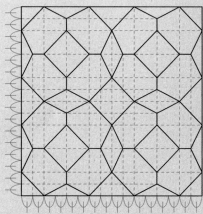

Tallahassee Block

Adorable patterns that look like
flowers. The central squares are
all made of vintage material, with
the upper left and lower right
pieces sewn from fabrics with
African prints.

Indian Chief

To avoid this huge piece from looking too bare, I used a material with an embroidered initial. The sense of presence gives it just the right touch. When connected to the rest of the image, it helps the sections with designs on them stand out.

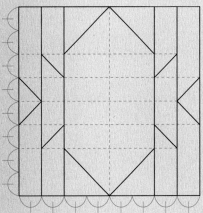

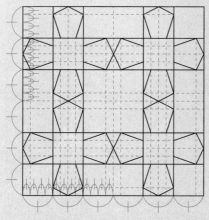

Smith Autograph Quilt

Depending on whether you choose to highlight the white sections or the printed sections, the impression given completely changes. I used darker hues in the printed sections, and the contrast this creates with the white part helps balance out the image.

Nine Snowballs

This pattern has an adorable name.
Another captivating possibility
is to sew several of these patterns
together, the four corner pieces
connecting up to expand the image.

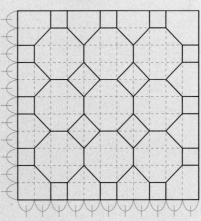

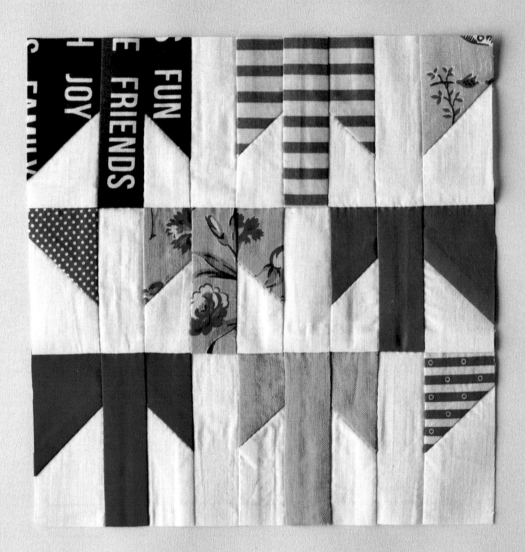

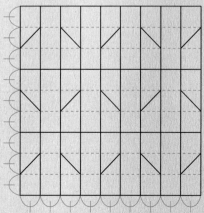

Mixed T

A pattern where upward Ts and downward Ts interlock. I chose colors that helped differentiate between the two kinds of T.

The Lover's Chain

By fitting the pieces together, the pattern becomes connected like a chain. I chose simple colors, white and red, with writing that can be seen in between the gaps.

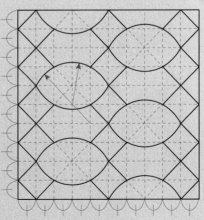

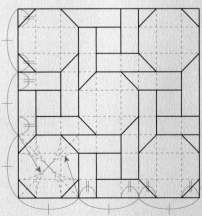

Twist Rope

This pattern interweaves with itself in a curious way that looks like a rope. It's also fun to insert print designs into those big piece slots.

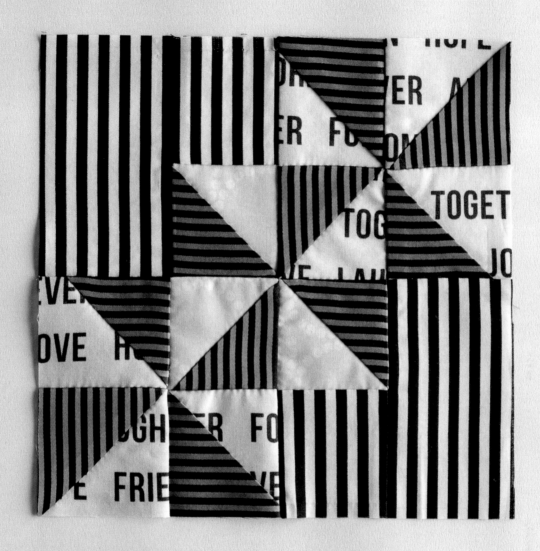

4th of July

The stripes give the pattern a sharpness and a sense of direction. We can either connect the windmill sections, or rotate them around, and both options open exciting new possibilities.

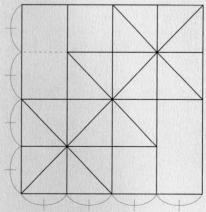

Circles and Quarter Circles

Patterns with even just a single circle in them look cute. Some of them require many pieces and complicated drafting and sewing procedures, so be attentive when working on them.

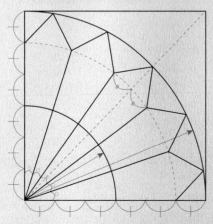

Fan Blades

This combination of blue and white for the background makes the whole look smart and very fresh. Among the quarter-circle patterns, this one uses a relatively big circumference.

Flo's Fan

It's crucial to take care when cutting the points of these sharp triangles. I added many different types of fabric, but I kept the color combination minimal to give it a chic look.

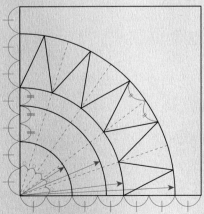

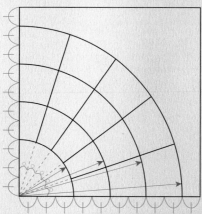

Lattice Fan

Here is a mix of flower designs, stripes, and polka dots. I chose printed designs that fit the size of each piece.

Texas

A Pop Art color scheme with intense tones. Make sure to get the striped designs to align with the direction of the star's spikes.

- There is a half-size pattern diagram on page 197.

You can use any width

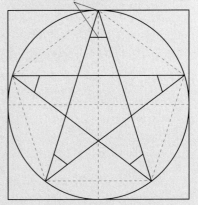

The appliqué circle can be
any width you want

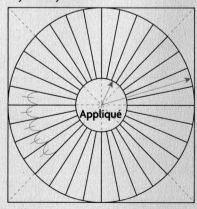

Signature

First, we sew the quarter blocks
and add them together later. By
adding alternating white spaces
to the color mix, the composition
looks cleaner.

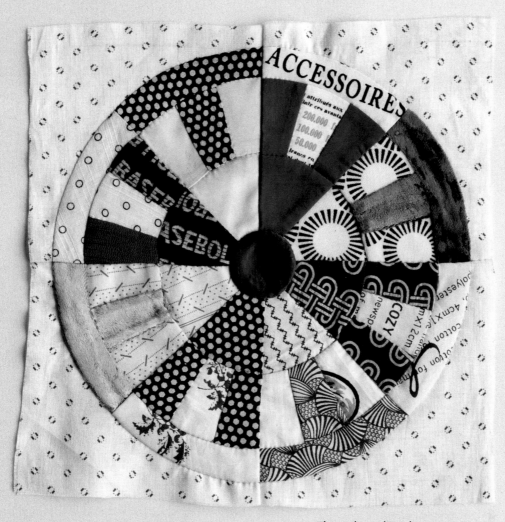

Wheel of Fortune

A pattern shaped like the wheel of fortune. By using velvet and other lush materials you can bring out changes in the pattern just by varying the texture.

The circle can be as large as you want

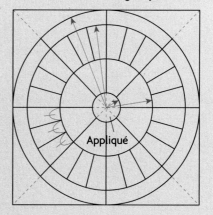

Appliqué

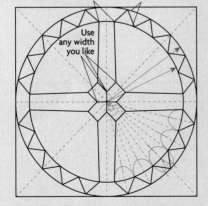

Use any width you like   Use any width you like

Use any width you like

Chips and Whetstones

I use an overall antique look to unify this image. The quarter circles are not sewn together, so they require inlay work.

- There is a half-size pattern diagram on page 198.

The circle can be as large as you want

Mariner's Compass

This is a complicated pattern with a lot of pieces, so I made it in a 9½" x 9½" (24 x 24cm) square. I chose different colors for each layer of spikes to help differentiate them.

- There is a half-size pattern diagram on page 198.

Appliqué

Choose any width you want

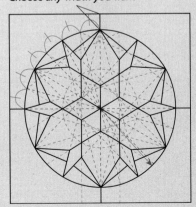

Texas Star II

A 9½" x 9½" (24 x 24cm) pattern. It includes a lot of sharp edges with complex shapes accumulated inside and outside the star's outline. I chose this color scheme to make the star more easily discernible.

- There is a half-size pattern diagram on page 199.

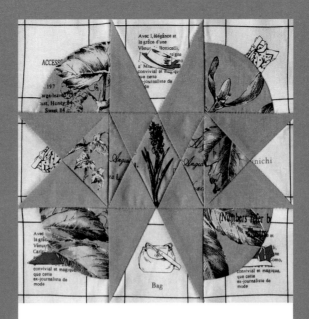

Patterns Divided by Block

Patterns made up of many separate blocks that are easy to analyze and divide. I've categorized them by their different applied uses. These patterns are comparatively easy to sew, since you simply make the blocks first and then connect them together.

Four-Block Patterns

These patterns can be divided by the middle into four blocks, and sometimes simply involve rotating around or mirroring just one or two of them.

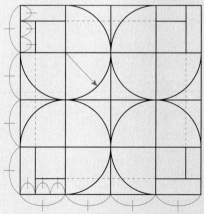

Alice's Patchwork

You can divide the central piece into four, as shown in the diagram, but if you're using the same piece of fabric, you can also keep it as one single piece, as shown in the photograph.

Corn and Bread

You can also unify the curved pieces into a single-color scheme. The bottom-right wool piece has some fusible web stuck behind it.

Give and Take

When all four blocks are connected, it forms a circle in the center. This pattern gives a different impression depending on whether you focus on the circles or the rhombi.

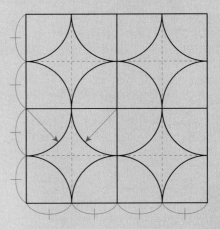

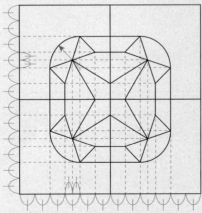

Oklahoma

Each block is the color negative of the other. This sort of negative color scheme really helps differentiate between the shapes.

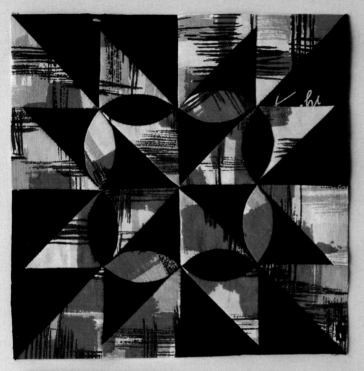

Fox Chase

Each quarter block is made of eight triangles, with every triangle being the color opposite of its pair. We then rotate these quarter blocks to create the full pattern.

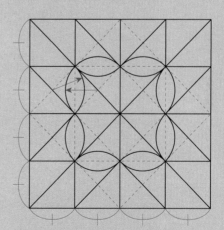

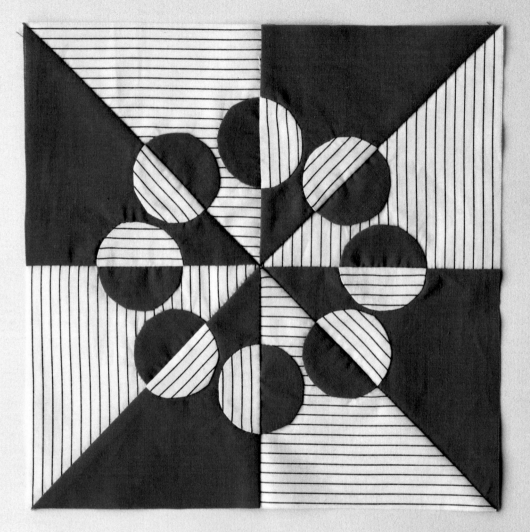

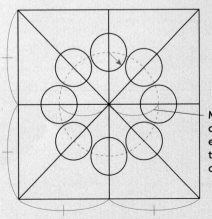

Make the circles small enough that they don't touch

Wonder of the World

I kept the color scheme simple to help distinguish the circles. I switched the directions of the stripes for the circles themselves and their background.

Bases Loaded

For this one, I used various subtle shades of pink. When sewing flower patterns all in the same direction, make sure you pay attention to the orientations of each piece.

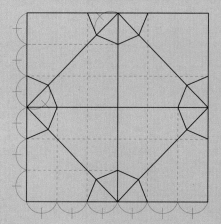

End of the Day

Uses a combination of yellow and blue. For the blue pieces, I used a white background with small patterns. For the yellow pieces, I used a white background with English print, which helps differentiate it from the other block.

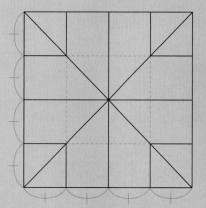

Choose any width you want

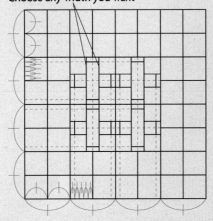

Checkerboard I

This pattern includes four crosses inside the checkerboard, which gives it a distinctive appearance. I used only plain color fabrics to keep it clean and neat.

Checkerboard II

This pattern includes a few octagons in the center. I used black and white, a classic combination for checkerboards, but made the center colorful to add some novelty.

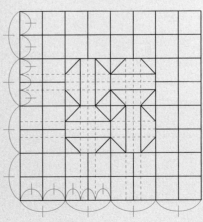

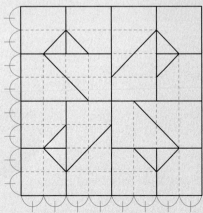

Colombian Puzzle

This pattern involves rotating the same block around four times. I gave these blocks some shared fabrics wherever they touched to add a feeling of continuity.

Coming Home

This pattern looks like a windmill, but it also looks like several arrows. By not using too many colors, we let the shapes be clearly visible.

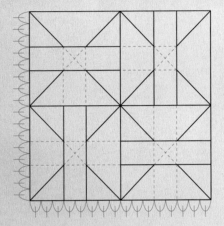

Left and Right

This pattern is also called Chevron. It's a simple shape, so I used the material's texture and design to add some originality.

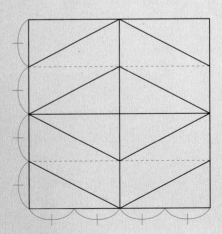

147

Pudding and Pie

I used different fabric designs for each block. It's hard to see, but if you look at the center, you'll see another windmill shape being created.

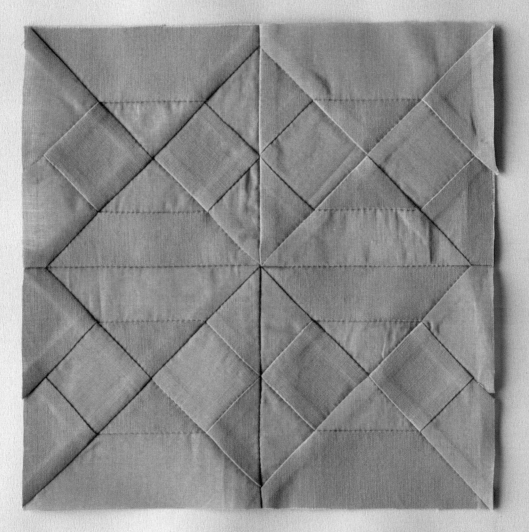

Winning Team

A pattern made from four blocks, each facing in the same direction but with a negative-image color scheme. Plain tone fabrics are perfect for negative-image layouts.

149

Spinning Wheel

The top example was made with just three different fabrics, whereas the bottom one shares only a single material among all four blocks. The top one allows the shapes to be clearly defined, while the bottom one is much more colorful and fun.

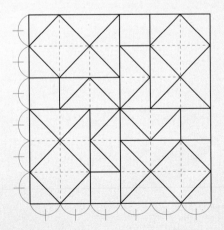

Salt and Pepper

A chic tone combination with mature sensibilities. It's a simple pattern, so I used high-quality and ridged materials to play with textures.

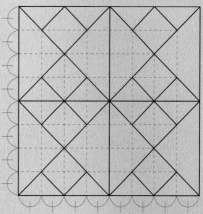

The Sprite

A pattern made from two types of blocks. For the lower example, I used Japanese-style silk crepe on the larger pieces. The Japanese material's color and texture adds a nice accent to the pattern.

Choose any width you want

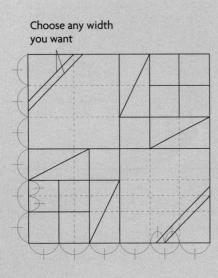

Identical Twins

Just like a reflection in a mirror, the top and bottom patterns are reversed. I've used old Japanese-style fabrics for the entire pattern.

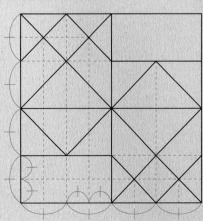

Blazed Trail

I chose a very light green print to help bring out the purple flower designs. It's a useful type of fabric since it's not completely plain, but it doesn't stand out, either.

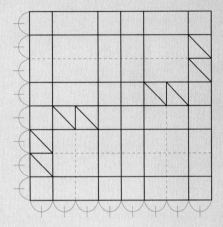

Tam's Patch

An easy-to-sew pattern that simply consists of squares. I used large-scale designs since they can be easily seen here.

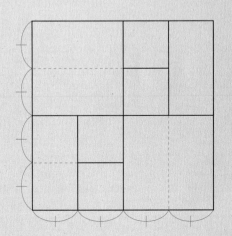

Nine-Block Patterns

These patterns can be divided into nine blocks and are created by rotating around or mirroring one, or even four, of them various times.

Beggar's Blocks

This pattern consists of one block positioned vertically and horizontally in succession. It's similar to other patterns called Spool and Bobbin.

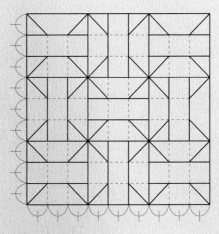

Nine-Patch I

A pattern with the simplest one-patch shape: the square. The white material includes white stripes reminiscent of handwriting.

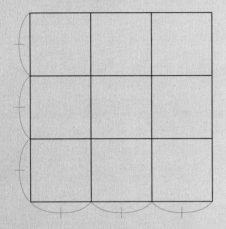

Nine-Patch II

I reversed the color scheme of the Nine Patch example above. Some of the plain white sections also include a background print, giving it a more complex look.

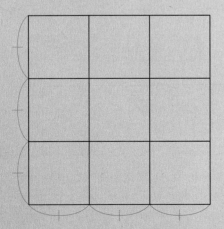

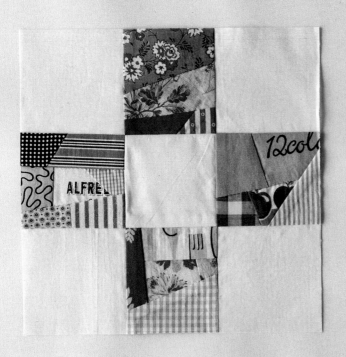

Nine-Patch Crazy Quilt

I arranged the designed sections of this pattern into a crazy quilt style (which involves cutting up the fabric freely). It also allows you to make use of cloth scraps.

Piece these sections in any way you like

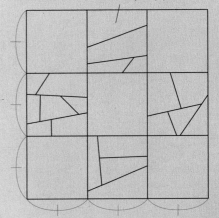

Nine-Patch Variation Original

I changed the vertical axis of the Nine Patch pattern by widening the central block. It ends up looking like a completely different pattern than the Nine Patch.

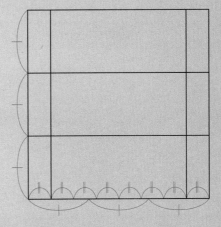

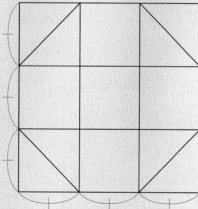

Shoofly

A pattern made only of squares and triangles. I only changed the direction of the top-left stripes to give it some sense of movement.

Triplet I

The name of this pattern implies a set of three. I used bottle green, a deep color, and white to create a sort of negative-image-tone scheme.

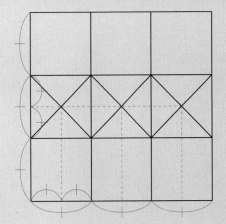

Triplet II

A pattern that shares the name with the one above. I used the same flower design for all the background pieces. This color scheme gives individuality to each of the three sections.

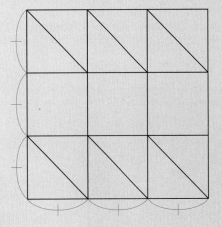

Kaleidoscope

It resembles an outstretched star made of spinning triangles.

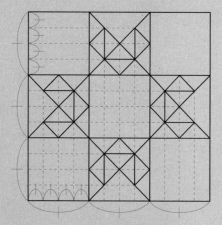

Rule Britannia

This has the same star shape as the above pattern, Kaleidoscope, but it is divided differently inside. I used light and dark tones—red, blue, and yellow—to give it a simple color scheme.

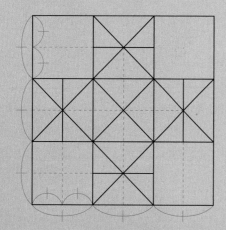

Nevada

I used only red and white here. By adding a small polka dot design, it suddenly looks a lot cuter.

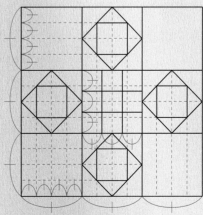

Dipsy Doodle

Compared to the overall size of the pattern, these triangle pieces are very small, so I used a lively red to emphasize them.

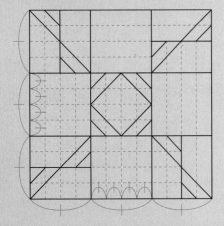

Nine-Patch Cross

A combination of blue and yellow, which are colors that go well together. I added stripes to the four corners, giving it the sense that it's expanding outward.

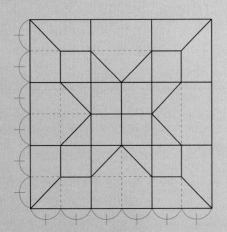

W. C. T. Union

The handwritten text is relaxing
but not too much. It gives it a
sense of movement that works as a
great accent.

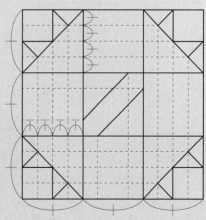

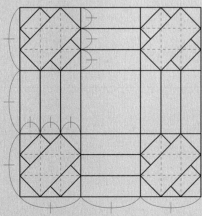

Dutch Puzzle

A fun thing about the pattern is how its blocks could potentially be interconnected outward further than this. I kept the color scheme simple, two colors, to help the shapes be discernible.

Indian Hatchet

A pattern named after a hatchet.
Applying the color scheme shown
in the picture gives it a sense of
rotating arrows.

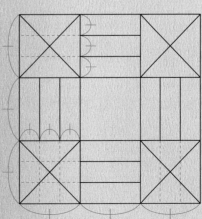

Appliqué

Blue Blazes

By mixing orange and deep blue, the pattern becomes serene. I made the plain fabric, polka dot, and flower design pieces share the same dark tone of blue.

Broken Circle

This pattern shows us a circle that
has broken up into pieces. By using
different fabrics for each piece,
we give it an even bigger sense
of movement.

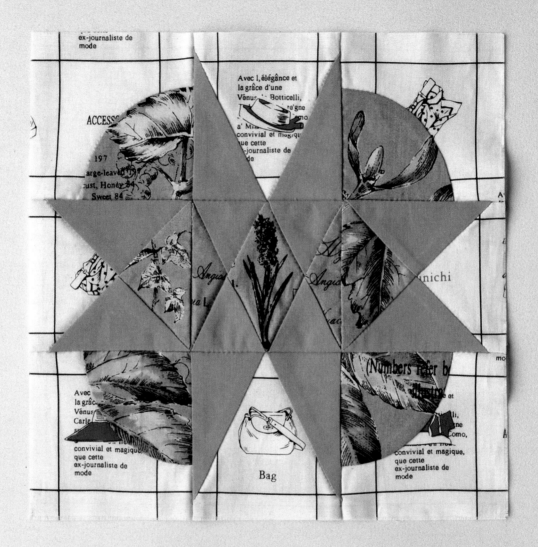

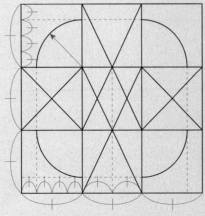

Bush's Points of Light

With this amber, I tried representing the shimmering of light. The intersection of curved lines and straight lines make it look as if this curious pattern is expanding.

Carnival

This is an arrangement of the classic Nine-Block-style pattern. I divided the blocks diagonally and then drew slanted lines from one to the other. It's a showy display, like a carnival would be.

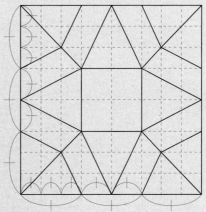

Central-Focus Patterns

These patterns are a mix between patterns with intersecting lines and patterns that converge in a central point.

Sew around the center

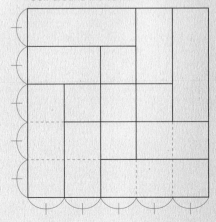

Crossing

We sew the rectangular blocks around the central square in a spiraling motion. If we then align the letters, we give the whole pattern a bigger sense of stability.

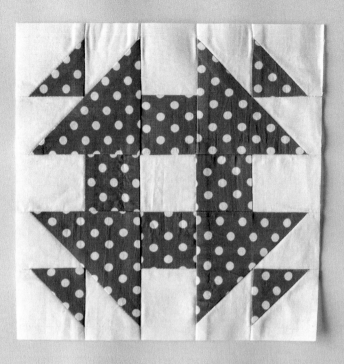

Monkey Wrench

A clearly defined pattern, divided into five portions. There are several other patterns with the same shapes but different ways of dividing them.

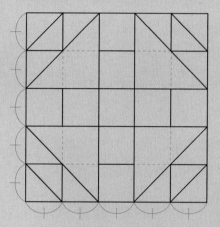

Double R

A pattern with a central rectangle divided into several shapes at each side. I gave a similar scheme to the left and right but added some variety by making the lower left a deep-green tone.

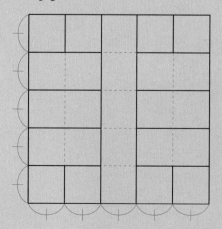

Star and Cross

I made the inner section red and light blue surrounded by designed fabrics. This pattern really highlights the central intersection.

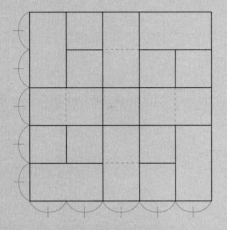

Tête-à-Tête

At first glance, it looks like a simple pattern divided into four blocks and a central zone. However, the blocks are divided into fine pieces.

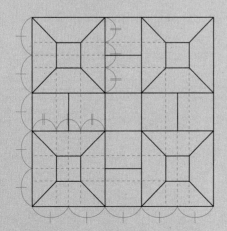

Fanfare

Four bands extend outward from the center, but they're each made of entirely different fabrics. The standard procedure with this pattern, however, is to craft the two outer pieces of each band with the same fabric.

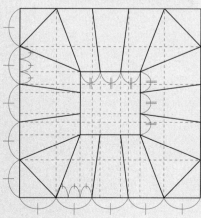

Nocturne

This pattern bears the name Nocturne, but it might also remind you of a windmill. I used a calm and soothing color combination.

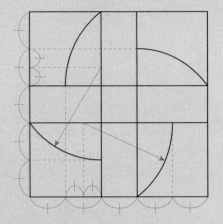

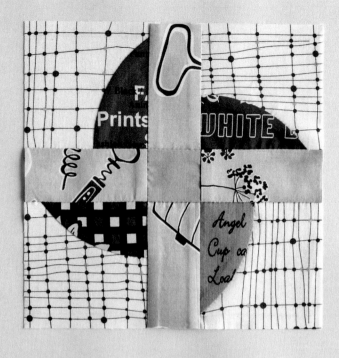

Sacrament

In the Christian faith, the word "sacrament" refers to divine grace. By switching colors at the intersections between curved lines, we give the pattern a more complex look.

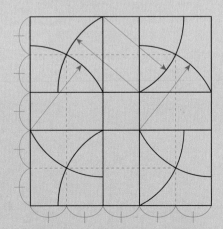

Lincoln's Platform

It's a pattern that is divided seven times into bands the same width as the central one. I tried to give each block distinctive fabrics while also retaining their unique shape.

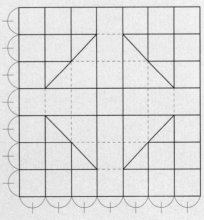

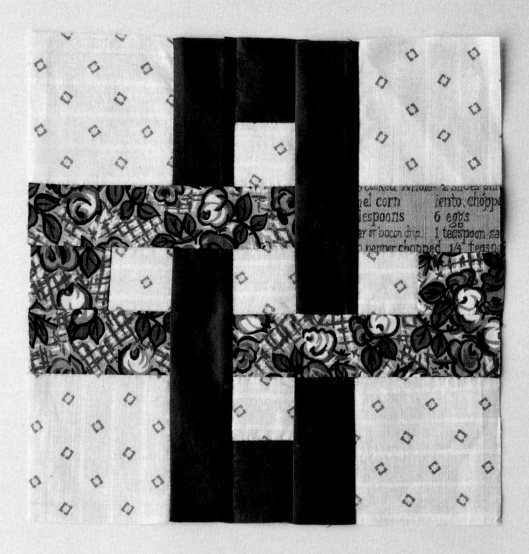

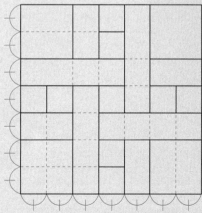

Chain Link

This pattern resembles a puzzle ring with its interlocking chains. I kept the colors simple to help distinguish the two chains.

Midsummer Night

I used stripes and plain fabric to balance out the other idiosyncratic fabrics. Be aware that the sides of the central octagon aren't all the same length.

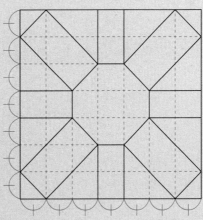

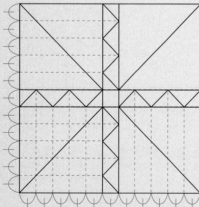

Fields and Fences

I used very striking prints for the top and bottom sets of three fabrics. When combining striking prints like these, it's crucial that an overall color and tone balance is kept.

How to
Make the Projects

- The unit of measurement used on the diagram is in inches. Use the conversion chart on this page as reference.

- The example photos and diagrams don't include the seam allowance in their dimensions unless specified. As a standard measure, the seam allowance is roughly ¼" (0.6cm) for piecing, ⅛" (0.3cm) for appliqué, and ⅜" (1cm) for construction. If the diagrams display cutting lines, you can cut at them without adding a seam allowance.

- Dotted lines with no text description represent seam lines, quilting lines, and stitching lines.

- Measurements for materials are indicated in fabric width and length. The actual length used should always be a little bit bigger. The measurements for the finished items are shown in vertical by horizontal sizes.

- When quilting, the pieces tend to shrink. Make sure you leave a sufficient seam margin in those cases.

- When creating the items, the final measurements may vary a little from the ones shown on the diagram.

Conversion Chart

in	cm	in	cm
⅛"	0.3	2¾"	7
5⁄32"	0.4	3⅛"	8
3⁄16"	0.5	3¾"	9.5
¼"	0.6	4"	10
9⁄32"	0.7	4½"	11.4
23⁄64"	0.9	5¼"	13.5
⅜"	1	5⅝"	14.3
½"	1.5	6¼"	16
¾"	2	7⅛"	18
1"	2.5	7¾"	20
1⅛"	2.85	11"	28
1³⁄16"	3	11½"	29.2
1⅜"	3.5	19¾"	50
1½"	4	23½"	60
2"	5	31⅛"	79
2¼"	5.7	39¼"	100
2½"	6	46¾"	119

Turtle Coaster

Pattern > page 57
Size of item: 4" x 4" (10 x 10cm)

Materials (for One Item)

Various fabrics for piecing and appliqué, fusible batting, backing fabric, and fusible web. For all materials, use a 6" x 6" (15 x 15cm) size.

Instructions

1. Create the main item's top section with piecing and appliqué.
2. Fuse batting to the pieced front and proceed to quilt it.
3. Fuse web to the back of the solid backing square. Place the prepared front and back together, aligning the edges. Stitch around the perimeter, leaving a 2" (5cm) opening for turning.
4. Turn right side out, press under the seam allowance at the opening, and hand stitch closed.

Piece four turtle blocks for main fabrics and cut four squares from backing fabric

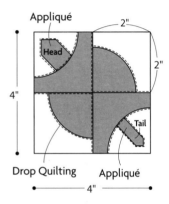

Adhere fusible fleece to the pieced block and fusible web to the backing fabric. The backing cloth should be the same size as the main body

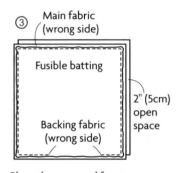

Place the prepared front and back together, aligning edges. Stitch around the perimeter, leaving a 2" (5cm) opening for turning

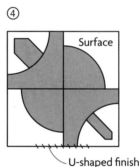

Turn right side out, press under the seam allowance at the opening, and hand stitch the opening closed

Real-size Pattern Paper

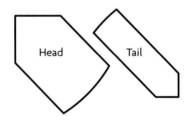

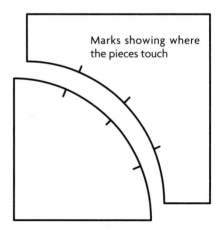

Marks showing where the pieces touch

I used the turtle sections of the Turtle I pattern and made coasters. With any pattern that divides into four sections, it's fun to try splitting them up.

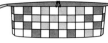

Pattern > page 156
Size of item: 2½" x 6" (6 x 15.5cm)

Important Reminders

• Remember to attach the zipper to the outside of the main body.

Materials

Various fabrics for piecing and zipper decoration, fabric for a medium-sized bag (including 15¾" [40cm] extra for a ½" [1.5cm] width bias tape), 9¾" x 13¾" (25 x 35cm) of batting, 9¾" x 7⅞" (25 x 20cm) of backing fabric with 7" (18cm) of length, and one two-way purse zipper (note: you will cut the zipper ends to size)

Piece one patchwork rectangle for main fabric as shown, and cut rectangle from backing fabric for inner bag.

Instructions

1. Piece together the top section.
2. Add the backing and batting to the top. Tack it and start quilting.
3. Fold the main body right sides together and sew both sides together. Sew the gussets at the lower corners as shown.
4. Repeat for the backing rectangle.
5. Fit the inner bag inside the main body, and baste around the top edge to secure. Place raw edges of bias tape to the top of the pouch and stitch around, stopping to join ends of tape before you finishing stitching to the pouch.
6. Trim the zipper if needed so that each end extends at least ½" (1.5cm) beyond the pouch sides. Place the wrong side of the zipper tape against the inside of the bias tape as shown and sew around the pouch opening, finishing as close to the zipper end as possible without folding the extended ends. Create a zipper stop if needed by stitching, and hand bar tack through the bias and zipper end.
7. Finish the zipper ends with folds of fabric as shown.

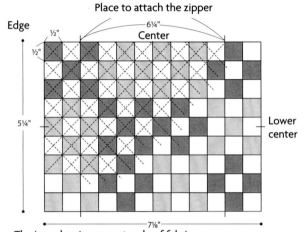

The inner bag is one rectangle of fabric

Instructions

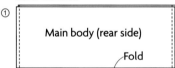

Fold the fabric in two, right sides together, and sew both edges
Sew the gussets
Sew the inner bag in the same way

How to Decorate the Zipper

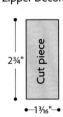

Two Sheets for the Zipper Decoration

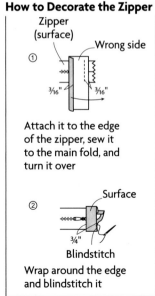

① Attach it to the edge of the zipper, sew it to the main fold, and turn it over

② Wrap around the edge and blindstitch it

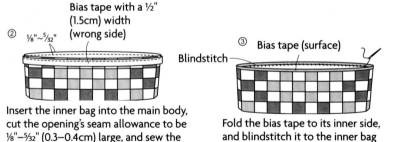

Insert the inner bag into the main body, cut the opening's seam allowance to be ⅛"–⁵⁄₃₂" (0.3–0.4cm) large, and sew the bias tape all around the main fold

Fold the bias tape to its inner side, and blindstitch it to the inner bag

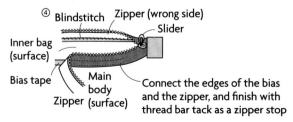

Attach the zipper to the bias tape, and apply a zipper stop with a thread bar tack.

I sewed together 108 square pieces, ½" (1.5cm) each. It's a cute pouch you can make even from little scraps of cloth you may have. I took two of the Nine-Patch patterns, and sewed them together in an alternating fashion.

Courthouse Steps Pouch

Pattern > page 94
Size of item: 4" x 5¼" (10 x 13.5cm)

Materials

Various fabrics for piecing, cotton batting, lining fabric, backing fabric, and fusible web. All should be 9¾" x 9¾" (25 x 25cm). Fabric for making the tie should be 2" x 21½" (5 x 55cm).

Important Reminders

- Remember to fold the backing fabric by joining the edges when sewing the main body's roll.

Instructions

1. Piece together the main body square.
2. Layer the lining and batting squares on the top, tack it, and begin quilting.
3. Create the tie as shown.
4. Place the main pieced square and backing square together, place the tie inside, and extend the raw end out from the upper left corner of the sandwich as shown. Pin and stitch around, leaving a 2" (5cm) opening at the bottom to turn.
5. Turn the pouch right side out through the opening and blindstitch closed.
6. Press up the three corners without and align as shown. Pin and hand stitch.

Piece one block for main fabric and cut squares for backing and lining

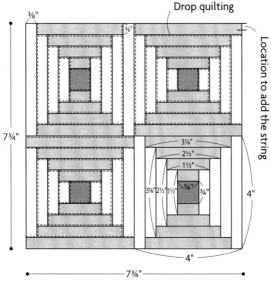

You need one square of backing fabric

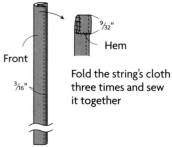

One Length of String

Instructions for the String

Fold the string's cloth three times and sew it together

Fold the edge of one side over three times and sew it

Instructions

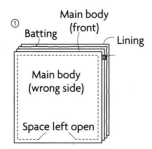

① Join the main body and backing fabric together, and sew the edges, leaving a 2" (5cm) opening for turning

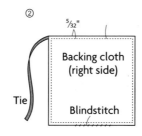

② Turn it to the front side, and blindstitch the open space

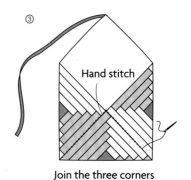

③ Join the three corners

I folded the Courthouse Steps pattern in an envelope shape to create a pouch. It's a stylish design that only requires you to fold or unfold it with the attached string.

Pattern > page 146
Size of item: 4" x 4" (10 x 10cm)

Materials (for One Coaster)

6" x 6" (15 x 15cm) of various fabrics for piecing, fusible batting, backing fabric, and fusible web.

Instructions

1. Piece together the coaster block..
2. Fuse batting to the wrong side of the block. Begin quilting.
3. Place the prepared block and backing right sides together. Stitch around all four edges, leaving a 2" (5cm) opening for turning.
4. Turn right side out, press under the seam allowance at the opening, and hand stitch closed.

Piece four blocks for the main fabric and cut four squares from backing fabric

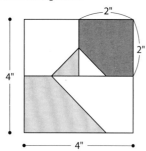

Fuse batting to the wrong side of the main body, and web to the backing cloth. The backing cloth should be a fabric of the same size

Instructions

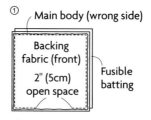

Join the main body and the backing, leave some space open, and sew the edges

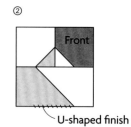

Turn right side out and close the open space

Real-size Pattern Paper

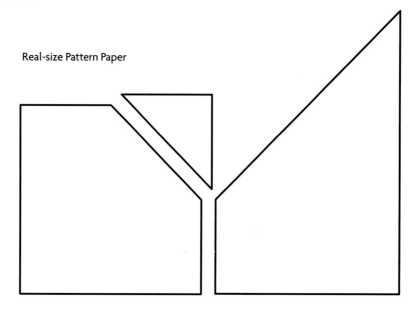

I divided the Colombian Puzzle pattern and used each quarter piece as a coaster. All four together create the complete pattern, but individually they become gorgeous coasters covered in geometric shapes.

Chainlink Quilt

Pattern > page 176
Size of item: 31½" x 47¼" (80 x 120cm)

Materials:

Various fabrics for piecing, 23½" x 51¼" (60 x 130cm) of fabrics for borders, 161½" x 1" (410 x 2.5cm) of bias for binding, and 35½" x 51¼" (90 x 130cm) of batting and backing cloth

Important Reminders:

- The bias used for binding must be cut in the same direction as the loom, making a striped pattern.
- The real-size diagram of the quilting lines is on page 199.

Instructions:

1. Piece together the top section.
2. Layer the quilt top, batting, and backing. Pin with quilting pins or tack to secure. Begin quilting.
3. Bind to finish, using your technique of choice.

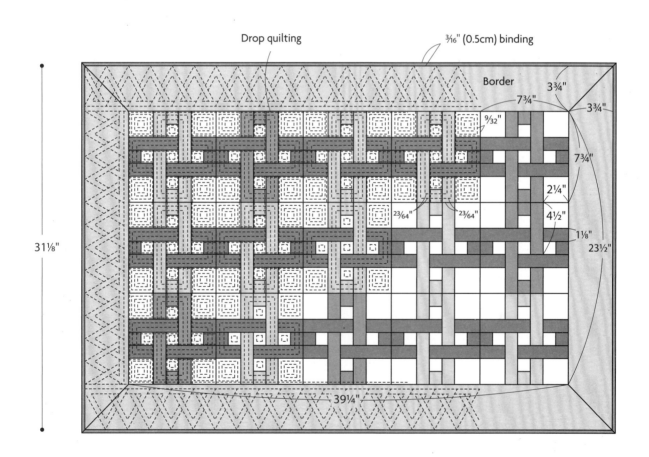

I made all the horizontal chains black for a unified style. However, I didn't forget to add a playful touch, making one of them white. It's a chic and elegant color combination.

—Sachiko Koyama

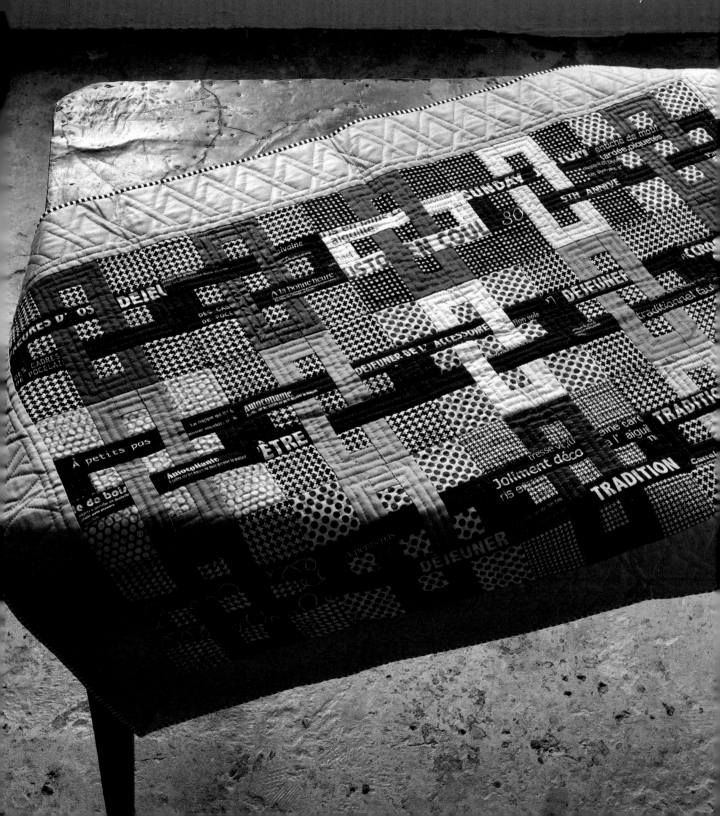

Pochette

Pattern > page 72
Size of item: 5¾" x 5¾" x 3¾"
(14.5 x 14.5 x 9.5cm)

Materials

Various fabrics for piecing, fabrics for the back side of the main body (which includes the bottom gussets, the zipper gusset, and the loops), 21¾" x 9¾" (55 x 25cm) of fusible batting, 9¾" x 9¾" (25 x 25cm) of batting, 17¾" x 9¾" (45 x 25cm) of lining fabric for the front and back of the main body, 27½" x 27½" (70 x 70cm) lining fabric (including the zipper gussets, the lining fabric for the bottom gusset, and 31½" x 1⁵⁄₁₆" [80 x 3cm] bias tape), a 10¾" (27cm) two-way zipper, a 53¼" x ⅜" (135 x 1cm) leather shoulder strap, and two D-shaped rings of ½" (1.5cm) width

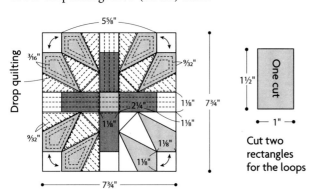

Piece one block for the main body

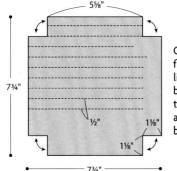

Cut one from flat fabric to line the main body, one for the bag back and one for the back lining

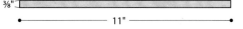

Cut two fabric and two lining for the zipper gussets

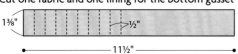

Cut one fabric and one lining for the bottom gusset

Important Reminders

- Fuse batting to the wrong sides of the back pieces, the zipper gusset, and the bottom gusset.
- Open the zipper before sewing the gussets onto the folded main body.
- Finish all the seam allowances with bias tape.

Instructions

1. Piece together the block for the main body. The lining of the main body should be cut from a single fabric.
2. Layer the main body, batting, and lining, tack or secure with quilting pins, and quilt. Repeat with the bag back and bottom gusset, omitting the batting, as these pieces were previously prepared with fusible batting.
3. Create the zipper gusset as shown.
4. Create two D-ring loops as shown. Right sides together, pin the short ends of the zipper gusset to the bottom gusset. insert the end of a D-ring loop to the right of the zipper on one side and to the left of the zipper on the other (the D ring loop will be sandwiched between the gussets), raw edges even. Stitch the gussets together, bind with bias tape, and blindstitch binding to the bottom gusset.
5. Sew the corners in the main body pieces front and back as shown. Insert the main body front in the gusset so that the zipper is centered across the top and raw edges are even. Pin and stitch all the way around. Repeat with the back side. Cover the seams with bias tape and blindstitch to the bag lining. Attach a purchased leather strap or create a fabric strap and attach to the D-rings with D-ring buckles.

Instructions

How to Sew the Main Body

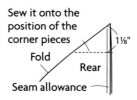

Sew it onto the position of the corner pieces

Join the arrows in the inner section and sew them. Sew the padded fabrics in the same manner

How to Make the Loop

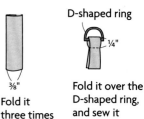

D-shaped ring

Fold it three times

Fold it over the D-shaped ring, and sew it

Continued on page 192

I used the Schoenrock Cross pattern and turned it into a pouch. I pinched the squares on each corner of the pattern to make gussets. The object's design is easy to make and makes good use of the pattern's many sections.

How to Create the Zipper Gusset

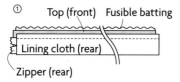

① Top (front) Fusible batting
Lining cloth (rear)
Zipper (rear)

Apply the fusible batting onto the top, and join the lining with the inner main body. Fold it over the zipper and sew it on

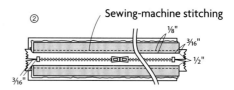

② Sewing-machine stitching
1/8"
3/16"
1/2"
3/16"

Turn it to the front and use a sewing machine to do the stitching. The zipper gussets for the opposite side are made in the same way

Instructions

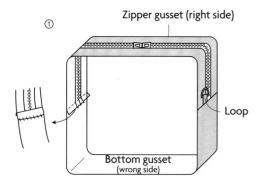

① Zipper gusset (right side)
Loop
Bottom gusset (wrong side)

Join the zipper gusset and the bottom gusset over each other, folding them over the loop, and sew it. Wrap bias tape around the seam allowance, and blindstitch on the bottom gusset

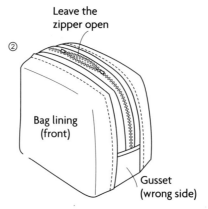

② Leave the zipper open
Bag lining (front)
Gusset (wrong side)

Join the main body and the padded fabric on the outside, then join the gussets onto the inside. Sew it all up. Wrap the seam allowance with bias tape

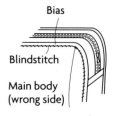

Bias
Blindstitch
Main body (wrong side)

The corners that wrap around the seam allowance should be flattened onto the main body's side and blindstitched

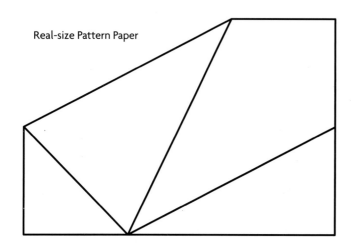

Real-size Pattern Paper

These diagrams are half-size reductions of 7⅞" x 7⅞" (20 x 20cm) patterns. If you wish to use them at 7⅞" (20cm), make sure to expand them to 200%.

page 31 Friendship Basket

page 35 Lily Original

These diagrams are half-size reductions of 7⅞" x 7⅞" (20 x 20cm) patterns. If you wish to use them at 7⅞" (20cm), make sure to expand them to 200%.

page 36 Basket of Lilies

page 41 Arkansas Meadow Rose

These diagrams are half-size reductions of 7⅞" x 7⅞" (20 x 20cm) patterns. If you wish to use them at 7⅞" (20cm), make sure to expand them to 200%.

page 45 Magnolia Blossom

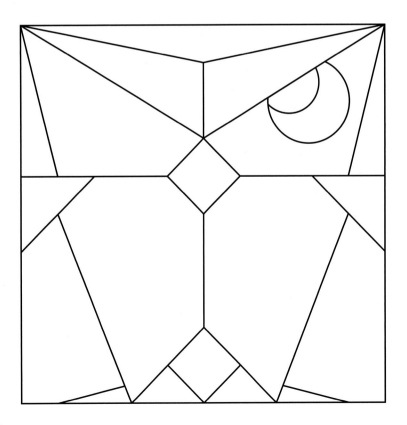

page 51 Georgia's Owl

These diagrams are half-size reductions of 7⅞" x 7⅞" (20 x 20cm) patterns. If you wish to use them at 7⅞" (20cm), make sure to expand them to 200%.

page 58 Turtle II

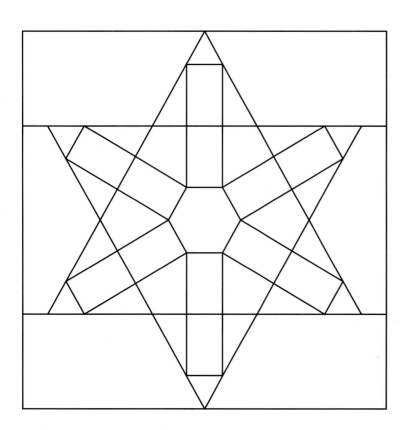

page 65 Wisconsin Star

These diagrams are half-size reductions of 7⅞" x 7⅞" (20 x 20cm) patterns. If you wish to use them at 7⅞" (20cm), make sure to expand them to 200%.

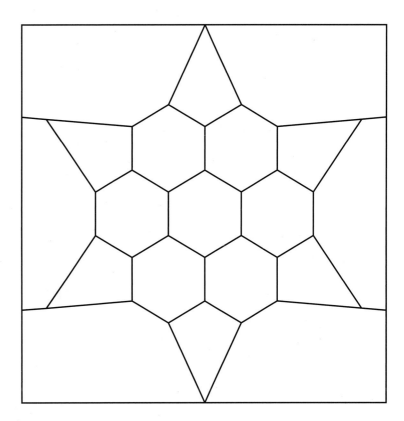

page 66 Grandmother's Star

page 131 Texas

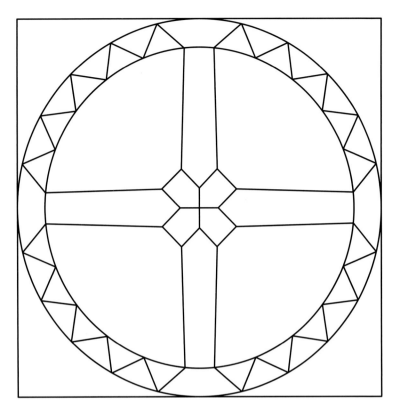

These diagrams are half-size reductions of 7⅞" x 7⅞" (20 x 20cm) and 9½" x 9½" (24 x 24cm) patterns. If you wish to use them at 7⅞" (20cm) or 9½" (24cm), make sure to expand them to 200%.

page 134 Chips and Whetstones

page 135 Mariner's Compass